Richard England

Editorial Director USA
Pierantonio Giacoppo

Chief Editor of Collection
Maurizio Vitta

Publishing Coordinator
Franca Rottola

Graphic Design
Alessandro Migliorato

Editing
Martyn J. Anderson

Colour-separation
Litofilms Italia, Bergamo

Printing
Poligrafiche Bolis, Bergamo

First published January 1998

Printed in Italy

ISBN 88-7838-028-8

Richard England

The Spirit of Place

Preface by
Maurizio Vitta

Introduction by
Richard England

Contents

Richard England,
as seen by Louis Hellman,
in his series 'Archi-Têtes'

Preface

Maurizio Vitta

In his fascinating book dedicated to the Mediterranean, Fernand Braudel writes that "you need to have been before you can be". There could be no better way of describing the Mediterranean sea and the lands and populations that thrive along its shores.

Richard England, a Maltese architect who lives on an island right in the heart of the Mediterranean, would certainly agree with Braudel's remark. As he himself is so fond of saying: "To create the future, build the past".

His idea of building is even more concrete than either history or culture. His works are really entrenched in the ground, and in stone, light and the physical-human landscape for which they are designed; his architecture inevitably tends to actually turn into earth, stone and light, burying itself in the landscape until they become one and the same thing.

There are, however, certain differences or modulations. England's idea of continuation coincides with evolution. The past acts as a starting point. The magnificent Megalithic remains that Malta still guards in the very heart of the island, the facades of its ancient churches and the layout of its Medieval ramparts are bound to capture our attention, but it is the true meaning of these remnants of a momentous history that needs to be perpetuated, the underlying sense behind a presence that has been around for a thousand years. Beyond these ancient structures, the present is projecting into the future with dynamic force.

England's architectural research has followed a winding course, without ever losing track of the basic direction in which it has been heading throughout all this experimentation. The various stages in his career can be singled out fairly clearly: from careful attention to the spiritual intimacy of site locations to powerful allusions to the functional layout of space; from a colourful sense of setting - creating an electrifying short-circuit between architecture and landscape - to great patience in adapting forms and structures to surrounding space; from an instinctive feel for history to great freedom of artistic expression.

Viewed in its entirety, England's work clearly tends towards what Paolo Portoghesi has described as "the theatre of architecture": the impact created by his shapes and colours tends to blend building and environment into a "memorable spectacle". Yet, as Portoghesi rightly points outs, "it is not so much the theatre that provides the key to deciphering England's designs, although it is often a powerful component in them, as a certain icastic force that characterises all his work. His works of architecture tend to play the part of a character with something to say and a firm belief in that something, interacting with the environment and, at the same time, creating an exception to it".

This is a lucid analysis. Relation and exception are two fundamental paradigms in all of England's work. The former creates a solid sense of permanent continuity; the latter calls this into question and creates that minimum displacement required so that the circularity of mere repetition is replaced by the branching ramification of history in all its vitality.

When England draws on his dazzling sketches depicting island locations in an attempt to break free from architectural design in search of an enlightening synthesis of graphics (or even painting), he is merely using these images to seek out a deeper concept, more basic model or archetype capable of justifying any variation. The process of design itself works in the opposite direction, but in the same basic sense. To begin with, it is the sketch that projects the emerging design into its spatial and, no less significantly, temporal setting. The environment is given, literally making its presence felt. Dialogue is the first step in the process of design, but the state of affairs grows more complex as soon as interaction is set up with the environment, both as it is and as it has been: to match up to its site location, the evolving work of architecture must enter into dialectical relation with it, negating its presence and breaking the rule to create the exception. This is the only way architecture can take on a sense of place, imposing itself as an ongoing reality like "a journey through the past, present and future", to quote the architect himself.

This is probably why Richard England's architecture often takes on theatrical connotations. But his own stylistic idiom is not just tied to setting: on the contrary, it is highly dramatic due to the way it both physically and materially embodies the conflictual nature of a work evolving in the present rather than trapped in the staticness of the past - eventually resolving this contradiction through a synthesis hovering on the brink of the future.

In all this, what might be described as "architectural culture" in its broadest sense, plays a crucial role, or in other words the results (however transient they might be) of the heated debate that has shaken the entire international architectural scene ever since the first cracks began to appear in modernity. Richard England certainly cannot be accused of sitting on the fence: his works take the side of those openly contesting modernism in the name of the latest design paradigms that have gradually emerged over recent times. He has avoided falling into the trap of "mannerism" - notably pointed out by Charles Knevitt, one of his keenest critics - by the original way in which he reads the kind of "regionalist" paradigm that has been so in vogue over the last few decades. Hardly surprisingly, a quote from Manfredo Tafuri fits him like glove: "remembering leads to tragic results: it brings out disputes from both the past and present, forcing us into a conflictual sort of composition through 'differences'".

The future takes us back to the past, but only through a kind of displacement that prevents the two from ever truly coinciding. The lesson to be learnt from contemporary architecture - to which Richard England makes his own original contribution - is summed up in this synthetic truth that provides ideological nutrition of great value for future projects, as well as stylistic guidelines on a strictly practical level.

Architecture + The Spirit of Place

Richard England

> "As you get to know Europe slowly ... you begin to realise that the important determinant of any culture is after all the 'Spirit of Place'."
>
> *Lawrence Durrell*

> "Modern Architecture is not built from some branch of an old tree, but is a plant growing directly from new roots."
>
> *Walter Gropius*

If Lawrence Durrell's words exalt the essence of place and cultural identity, Walter Gropius' statement emphasises modern architecture's blind commitment to a reductive rationalism devoid of any form of attachment to the past or its memory. It is because of this dissociation and distaste for the past and its traditions that the universal took over from the particular, in the lean years of the so called International Style. In reducing architecture to a few limited universal truths this movement curtailed the impacts and interactions forthcoming from both place and past in the then current architectural interventions. Architects at the time consequently spent too much time studying joints in buildings, most of the time forgetting the most important joint of all, that of the building to its site and surroundings.

In contrast, my ideology of architecture (since the beginning of my career) is one related specifically to place, based on a philosophy of "a new leaf instead of a new tree". The projects illustrated in this monograph are a selection from three decades of my "making" of architecture mostly within the limited confines of my native Maltese Islands. All these buildings use the cultural identity of the Islands as a spring-board for the creation of an architecture born from climate, history and tradition, and which, in its final built-form, becomes both a symbol and celebration of the essential "spirit of place".

Genius Loci

> "To know a place one must know its memories."
>
> *Richard England*

The Maltese Islands measure a mere 320 square kilometres. They lie like a scorched leaf in the centre of the Mediterranean sea. The sole building material available is the natural rock of which these islands are composed. Throughout its history, this archipelago offers a valuable example of the intelligent use of this material. Through the unity of this ethnic stone, a strong sense of continuity and homogeneity is evident in the vast overlays of man's activities over many centuries in a struggle to wrest a living for survival in an environment of limited and restricted resources. The stone which is quarried from a sedimentary rock formation is a globigerina limestone. It is golden in colour, easily cut, dressed and worked.

A visit to these quarries is a rewarding visual experience. The piling of cube upon cube of the quarried ochre blocks evokes images of the constructed complexes and it requires little imagination to crystallise these unit groupings into the cluster-forms of the buildings of tomorrow; a relationship which emphasises the strong organic link between the material utilised and the form of completed buildings.

Because of their strategic position at the cross-roads between the two great traditions of Europe and the Islamic world, the built expression of the Islands is a strong reflection of the meeting place of the different multi-cultural overlays which have dominated them throughout history. Here is a synthesis of not only East and West but also North and South. The traditional close-knit cubic townscape clusters, echoes of the Island's Arab occupation, are crowned by soft rounded domes of Baroque churches imported through the Italian and Spanish influences of the Order of St. John of Jerusalem. The synthesis of these two cultures, provides the essence of identity which crystallises the "Spirit of Place" of these islands. It is interesting to note a similar locational cross-cultural parallel in linguistic terms. Malta's own language is of Semitic origin and sound but written in the Roman alphabet.

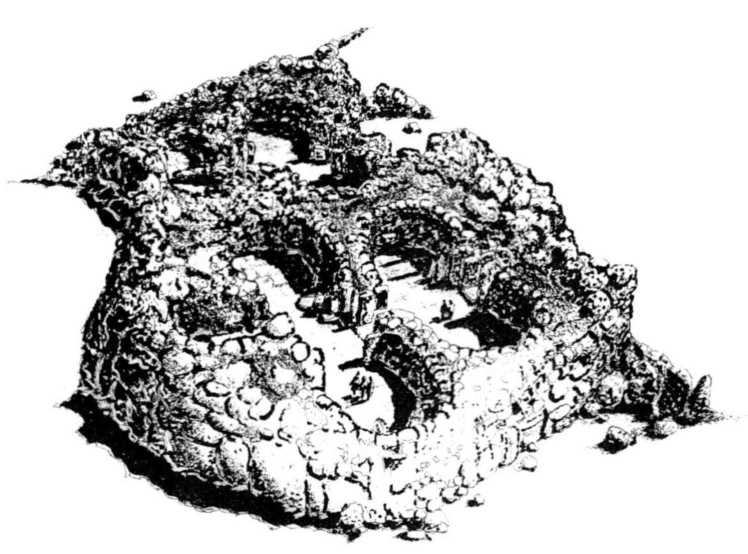

This land is an architectural context of maximum utilisation of minimal resources. One is aware of a total utilisation of the limited available materials and their means. The fields are built, the soil accumulated between the rubble walls and much that appears natural is, in fact, man-made. In a strange manner, this place, through its rich history-laden development has continually remodelled its rocky self in response to the specific needs of its inhabitants at different times. In Malta, perhaps more than anywhere else, the sum of the parts is actually equal to the whole. Constantly, stone is being hollowed out, cut away and built-up to suit man's requirements. What is there has always been there, it is just that some of it has been remodelled. In contrast to the ochre-coloured stone environments, this island is also enriched with vibrant colour expressions which manifest themselves in ethnic boats, festa and fireworks. It is this combination of monochromatic buildings and colourful outbursts which characterise the totality and essence of the place. Worthy of particular notice are the vast series of Megalithic temple structures dating back to over 3000 BC. These anthropomorphic structures, indicate the islands in pre-history as probably the Holy Shrine of the Middle Sea. With their deft spatial organization, these time-resisting giant stone buildings, man's earliest built evocations to an Earth Deity, have been a constant inspiration and influence throughout all my working life.

Design Methodology

> "What is new and essential must of necessity be grafted to old roots."
>
> *Bela Bartok*

If one is born and bred in such an environment it is only natural that one should produce an architecture which relates specifically to, not only the visual qualities of the place, but also to its complex tradition and history. It was William Blake who said, "We become what we see". This inborn ethnic culture was supplemented by more sophisticated overlays acquired during a study-work period in the Milan Studio of the Italian architect-designer Gio Ponti.

Since the early period of my creative architectural life, I have always believed in an expression of an architecture as a process of *evolution* as opposed to *revolution*. I have never believed that one should bring in the new at the expense of the old. Earlier in this century, as referred to above, architects turned their back on the past, declaring in dogmatic terms that they were totally independent of its heritage and that their belief was only in the development of technology. Consequently buildings were no longer tied to specific places, materials and history.

Architects, in attempting to wipe out the past, came frighteningly close in succeeding to create a universal solution to what was never a universal problem. In this process of international industrialism, man ceased to be an individual and became an anonymous cipher. Today, however, as man becomes even more mobile in an ever-shrinking global-village civilisation, he is developing an increasing awareness and necessity for the values of roots. It is an essential truth that these values are recognised not

only as a vital psychological need, but more so, as an essential equation to successfully relate mankind to a basic socio-cultural existence and location in a time-space framework.

The basic failure of most of the architecture of the 20th Century must however be attributed, not to the dogmas of Modernism, but more specifically to those of Internationalism. The demands of the Modern Movement, unlike those of Internationalism, could well be adapted to an architecture rich in a search for meaning and content in specific context. Within the parameters of a philosophy of continuity within change, I have always attempted to graft my buildings to ethnic roots, in the process manifesting my belief that architecture must relate to and evolve from the "Spirit of Place", but also always be contemporary in its expression.

In all my buildings I have tried to obtain results which are technologically progressive, yet culturally conservative, in the sense that to "conserve" means to keep alive. Technology is part of the answer but so also is history. I have tried to evoke within contemporary design methodologies, the essential qualities of the places I build in and their heritage in an architecture which reflects the formal essence and identity of the place, and in the process, I have attempted to transfer tradition and roots from the position of a silent conscience to that of a central topic of debate. In all my works, the site, or *genius loci* has been the initiator of the whole creative process. The location must always be regarded as the springboard for the whole design process, not only in terms of its *physical data* (geography, topography, climate and materials), but also its *memory data* (tradition, culture, legend and history), for it is not only what is visible that is important but more so the "present absences" and "absent presences" of a place, which are also inherent properties of identity.

Architecture is about listening to and understanding this data at a specific moment in time. I therefore work on these generators in a collective, rational and intuitive manner, in such a way as to mix "knowing" with an equal capacity to "forget knowing"; a reminder that to acquire sophistication requires spontaneity. The element of time brings into focus the "physical" and "memory" databanks, and provides the current technologies, social movements, political and economical aspirations of the place. These "voices of a site" provide pointers towards valid solutions to the particular problem. They will tell the architect whether the environment is weak and therefore requires him to be strong, or they may tell him that the environment is strong and that he is to be docile. Wherever an architect works, he needs hands that see and eyes that feel. The most essential quality for any architect attempting to produce an integrated tapestry of time and place woven into a fabric of identity remains above all an essential dose of good manners.

The Maltese Islands from the early sixties had already begun to rely on tourism as the major aspect of their economy. The housing of these travelling masses poses problems of accommodation, and consequently the majority of my buildings of that period focus on providing solutions to this end. Tourism, very much a speculator's market, if not controlled becomes one of

man's worst forms of 20th Century pollution. The problem of how to accommodate masses of people without committing environmental suicide in the process, together with the preservation and development of the ethos and logos of their target areas, is the architect's prime concern and responsibility. Together with these essential factors the architect must consider the qualities of the "Genius Loci" of the region he is building in, which in tourist buildings becomes one of the "materialistic" functional requirements. It is this very different and particular "Spirit of Place" which attracts the tourist in the first place. It was George Bernard Shaw who said, "I dislike feeling at home when I am abroad".

The pioneer path-finder in architecture's quest for an expression of place, Hassan Fathy, taught us that "tradition is not necessarily synonymous with stagnation." Later it was pioneer practitioners like Rifat Chadirji in Iraq, Aris Konstantinidis in Greece, Geoffrey Bawa in Sri Lanka, Faraoui and De Mazieres in Morocco, and of course, Luis Barragan in Mexico, who attempted to create an expression of contemporary architecture based on historical and traditional roots which crystallised the potential of their respective regions and in the process connected buildings to both their physical and cultural backgrounds. In my own buildings, my quest has always been directed towards attaining the optimum for local culture, drawing the best of tradition together with scientific Modernism, and in the process treating the delicate fabric of the particular site with respect and humility.

All my works attempt a conscious and intuitive blending of traditional forms and scale requirements of the region, together with its history and symbolic past in direct quotation, allusion or metaphor, in conjunction with a modern approach and use of techniques and materials. The main object is to obtain an expression particular to its location, while evoking a strong sense of identity. Collectively this body of works attempts to demonstrate my belief that the essential act of architecture is to understand the vocation of the particular place one is building in, and in the process discovering what the place wants to become. All these projects reflect my determined effort to develop a climatologically responsive architecture that above all enhances the character of the site.

In the second period of activity (1980-1990), while the concept of the "Genius Loci" is still strongly maintained in direct quotation or metaphor, there is a strong infusion and overlay of the sense of the poetic. This is a stage characterized by my search for a metaphysical architectural expression influenced also by the literary writings of Calvino, and the pictoral world of such artists as De Chirico, Delvaux and Magritte. The third creative period tends to bring together a combination and extension of the earlier design methodologies. However, the return to a more direct and straightforward approach in contrast to the complexity of the second stage is manifested in such works as the University of Malta extension, the Central Bank of Malta and the Church of St. Francis of Assisi at Qawra. It was Axel Munthe who said "the soul needs more space than the body". My search for poetic content in architecture is further emphasized in the body of sacred spaces where my research evolves into a faith-oriented methodology of approach to create spirit-laden arenas of meditation and silence.

Conclusions

> "Tradition is the alphabet
> Form is the language
> Architecture is the poem."
>
> *Richard England*

My current philosophy of approach further convinces me to believe that ultimately architecture is about making buildings and that when all is said and done what remains is the building. I am now very much for an architecture that excludes "isms" (note how quickly they become "wasms"), avoids pigeon-holing (uncomfortable unless you happen to be a pigeon), and focuses instead on a sense of appropriateness to not only time and place, but to climate, tradition, memory, geography, history and context together with culture and above all to its users from both a materialistic and emotional aspect.

The incestuous interbreeding of Post-Modernism, where quotations from the past were rewritten as fiction (I confess to having had a one night stand with this Movement), together with the hedonistic self-indulgent ego-centricity of Deconstructivism are exercises which the profession would do best to avoid. What is required is to denounce current obsessions with novelty, for novelty's sake, and to acknowledge and respond to more lasting and stable values. Architecture needs roots as much as it needs foundations. The prime requisite remains, above all, that a building is both "appropriate" and relevant to its surroundings and its time. Through architecture one should have an understanding of where one comes from and where one is going to. Architecture is about making man, not only physically, but also emotionally, comfortable. Architects must learn to give back a sense of belonging to the space which makes and surrounds their buildings. Architecture must be creation, not just industrialism, and must ultimately focus on the emotional human factor, for it is above all, in the words of Emilio Ambasz, "an art involved in giving poetry to the pragmatic".

Architecture is about ordered space, which, besides serving the essential materialistic functional requirements, must also be capable of causing an emotive response in man (vide Luis Barragan's poetic creations). My creed is for a contextual architecture that is an expression of a symbiosis of past and present. It must serve not only function (the architect's task starts once behavioural needs have been met), but also meaning. This meaning is a simulacrum of a hidden multiplicity of signs, moulded into a stimulating architectural language, which looks to and learns from both local culture and global civilisation. Architecture for me is the joining of head and heart in a joyous response to life. It requires a pluralistic approach, incorporating the amalgamation of the surprising and the familiar, recalling old images and concepts from memory, and involving them with the new, in order to provide both with an enriched and extended identity.

I firmly believe that the new, if it is to be valid, can only be built on the past, and that every architectural gesture should have history as its source and utopia as its end.

In seeking to create an architecture that is situational as opposed to universal, individual as opposed to collective, and unique as opposed to standardised, the architect of today must strive to rediscover the meaning of such words as beauty, magic, silence and enchantment. These are pre-requisities for creating an expression which synthesises and amalgamates the poetic and the pragmatic. The ultimate role of the architect is, I believe, to make the ordinary extraordinary in the environmental context of the place and time in which he is building. It was Tenessee Williams who said "I don't want reality, I want magic".

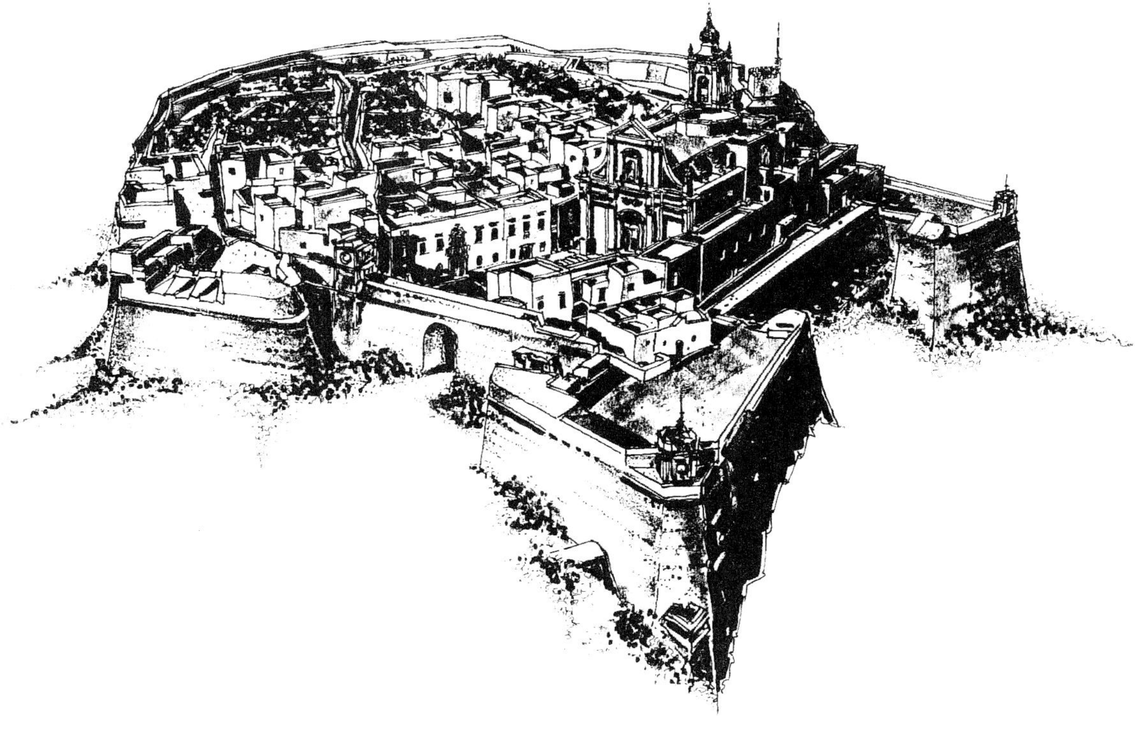

Early Works

Identity, Locality, Continuity

"An architecture of evolution not revolution."

Richard England

In the early sixties when Richard England started his architectural career, architects in the world were involved in a rationalisation of production and realisation of buildings which seemed to exclude aesthetic, emotional and ethnic qualities.

In contrast, Richard England's early works already demonstrated a deep-rooted understanding and personal commitment to the patrimony of his island home. His hotels and other tourist buildings of this period successfully re-interpreted traditional forms in a thoroughly modern manner using indigenous materials to produce buildings which were responsive to the environment of their origins and to their location in time.

Charles Knevitt, in his book on England's architecture "Connections" (Lund Humphries London 1984), writes "he took what modern technology had to offer, combined it with the traditions of the past to produce an architecture which was a living contribution to the present. In all these works the architect's main concern is with identity, locality, continuity and symbolism." Most of all England's buildings had to do with appropriateness and belonging.

In the Ramla Bay Hotel and the Ta' Monita Tourist Village it is the imposition of the former and the integration of the latter into the surrounding terrain that impress, while in the private villa La Maltija and the Dolmen Hotel, it is the sheer robustness of the buildings and the many allusions to his island's pre-historic past which are characteristic.

In the Dolphin Court Apartments there is an obvious reference to the informality of Mediterranean seaside architecture, while the Cavalieri Hotel rising from the water's edge displays rows of an ordered but seemingly random pattern of square and arched openings which extends and echoes the rhythm of the adjacent cubic fishermen's houses.

In the Salina Bay Hotel, England achieves a complete manifestation of what he calls "the most important joint of all, the joint between building and site." Here he takes the visual metaphor of the walled city to create a fortress-like structure which while dominating successfully integrates itself into its surroundings.

The Festaval Tourist Village on the North part of the Island, terraces itself into the sloping landscape so that at no point does the building project more than one floor in height above the contours of the existing site.

This discreet insertion offers total integration of building into site taking its cue from the existing topography of the surrounding cascading field walls.

In the well-mannered arched facade of the Marina San Gorg Tourist Complex, Richard England pays well-mannered homage to the grammar of the close by British-built barrack blocks. Chris Abel has written that "it is a beautifully sited and noble kind of building, rare qualities in themselves for any tourist establishment." (*Transformations-The Architecture of Richard England*, Mid-Med Bank Ltd., Malta 1987). Here, the old and the new are happily married in composition and material.

In all of these projects, England's design methodology fuses together tradition and topography in early manifestations of the architect's respect for the heritage of his land. Many of these buildings have since been changed, added to or demolished. Few examples of England's work of this period remain unadulterated.

Opening page, detail of Ramla Bay Hotel, Marfa, Malta, 1964.
Left, Dolphin Court Apartments, Ta'Xbiex, Malta, 1964.

Right, Villa la Maltija, Naxxar, Malta, 1966.

Dolmen Hotel, Qawra,
Malta, 1966.

Left, Mid-Med Bank Computer Centre, Qormi, Malta, 1968. Opposite page, Cavalieri Hotel, St.Julians, Malta, 1968.

Detail of Ta' Monita Tourist Village, M'Scala, Malta, 1968.

Salina Bay Hotel, Salina, Malta, 1970.

Salina Bay Hotel, Salina, Malta, 1970.

Festaval Tourist Village, Mellieha Bay, Malta, 1980.

Marina San Gorg Tourist Complex, St.George's Bay, Malta, 1980.

Major Works

Church of St. Joseph

Manikata, Malta
1962 - 1974

"From the sound of stone,
comes the silence of space."

Richard England

The design and building of Manikata Church on a hill top in the centre of a small hamlet provided the architect with his first opportunity to demonstrate that for architecture to have real meaning, it must function at many levels. Placed on the crest like a large abstract sculpture, moulded in sensuous curves, the Church provides interesting solutions, not only on a formal level, but more so on the equally important strata of religious and social interactions.

Unhappy with the official church hierarchy of the time, the architect attempted to design a sacred space modelled instead on dialogue and equality between the celebrant and the congregation. The autocratic image of a local remote deity had to be recast into a new image celebrating above all, a spirit of joy. The Church, in Richard England's mind, was to be read more as a house of the community than one of the deity.

In terms of architecture, society and religion, Manikata was to be above all a contemporary statement, but one which also spoke in the vernacular language. Introducing these changes to the Baroque-ridden attitudes of the Maltese Islands of the early sixties was no mean task. However, contemporary to the preparation of the designs for the Church, the second Vatican Council issued new directives on church art and architecture, and these liturgical reforms helped to get the project approved by the church authorities.

Twelve years in the making (the Church was eventually inaugurated in 1974), Manikata became a symbol of a new spirit, but at the same time one which strongly evoked and recalled its origins and background. It drew its inspiration from the island's two golden ages of religious architecture, those of the Earth Goddess Megalithic Temples of pre-history, and the ornate opulent Baroque which had dominated the Island for the last five centuries. This place of gathering, carved in a contemporary Christian language also related to and originated from lesser local traditions and building typologies, such as those of the rural toolshed dry-wall constructions known as "girna". These forceful images are combined together and injected with a relevance suitable to a 20th Century church in order that it could act as a bridge between Malta of the past and that of the future, yet simultaneously very much of both. This *relevant* borrowing of ethnic-rooted forms produced a space of relaxed informality which pointed more towards a place for family gatherings than that for solemn religious ceremonies.

Progress, however, was slow and difficult, funds were limited (the whole church cost under $50,000) and the volunteers and small labour force available fluctuated. Although full working drawings were prepared, these proved to be virtually useless as the local village voluntary workers could not read drawings. However, what initially appeared to be a negative aspect and major stumbling block, subsequently provided Richard England with a personal experience which radically changed his whole approach to architecture. In order to ensure progress on site, a vital personal involvement followed in the actual building of the Church, in almost a medieval manner. The architect usually only prepares "means to an end", in as far as he is only concerned with the preparation of drawings and documents, and not the actual *making* of the building itself. This involvement in the building process had a lasting effect on England's future understanding of the whole architectural process and he learnt to believe that "every architect, at least once in his lifetime, should make a building with his hands". Manikata was indeed a building fashioned by human hands; a living manifestation of the villagers' commitment, belief and creed; a building built for the people by the people, a specific architecture for a specific place, in a specific time: a Church for today, designed on the foundations of yesterday.

This project was awarded the Interarch Laureate Prize in 1985.

Text based on Chris Abel's essay in Manikata Church, *Academy Editions, London 1995.*

Preliminary sketch.
Below, entrance porch.

View of church
and piazza.

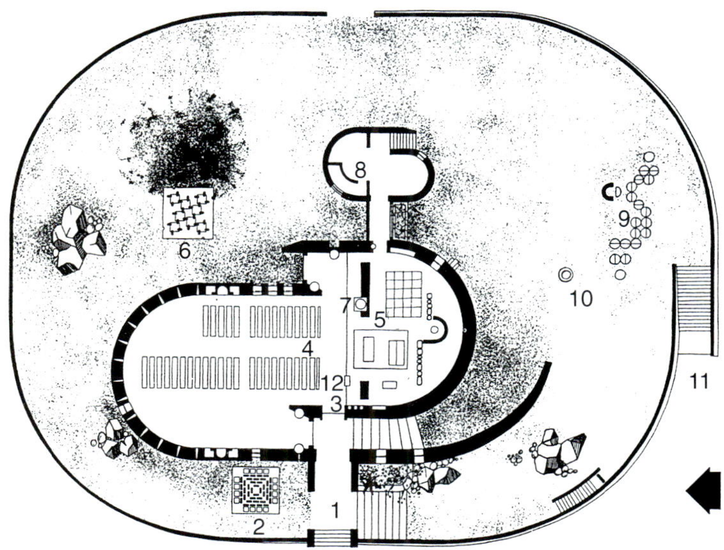

Plan of church
and surrounding area.

1. Main entrance porch
2. *Labyrinth City* sculpture
3. Cross
4. Nave
5. Sanctuary
6. *City of Towers* sculpture
7. Baptisimal font
8. Sacristy
9. Belfry and outside seating
10. Base of sundial
11. Access to zuntir
12. Lectern

Detail of the perimeter wall of the church.

Opposite page, the *City of Towers* sculpture.

The Belfry and outside seating in the southern part of the complex. Above, the interior.

A Garden for Myriam

St. Julians, Malta
1982

"Do we discover
or do we invent architecture ?"

Richard England

In ancient days, architects were white magic practitioners involved in the making of environments concerned with the rituals and myths of man in relation to his particular location in place and time. In even earlier times, the builders of the sacred spaces of that era were conversant in the secret knowledge of celestial bodies and proficient in the understanding of the Oriental terrestrial sciences of Feng-Shui and Kaso. This cognitive learning manifested itself in examples of cultured buildings, allowing architecture, throughout prehistory to be considered not only a creative enactment but also as a path to enlightenment.

Designers and builders have continued this tradition in time, to strive and create the equivalent concrete realities of the literary-fashioned dreams of such romantic authors as Homer, Swift, Verne, Carroll, Tolkien, Borges and Calvino. Real places of such chimerical qualities as Petra, Athos, Carcassone, Saana, Kathmandu and Kyoto, more than equal the legendary morphological creations of such fabled territories as Ogiga, Avalon, Lemuria, Atlantis, Wonderland, the Middle Earth and Zenobia.

Both the actual and literary creations of these spaces of legend manifest man's inherent yearning for places of poetic content, reminiscent of his original lost paradisal-terrestial lot. All of these trance-like spaces have something of the qualities and properties of magic to enable them to be referred to, above all, as places of meaning and poetry. Unfortunately, the 20th Century has been responsible for the removal of many of these qualities, together with much of the sense of "wonderful", from our every-day lives. Sterile rationalist thought-patterns have involved man in the constant stripping down of the essential magical content of things.

A Garden for Myriam was conceived by Richard England to counteract this approach and is created in the spirit of the lost tradition of non-utilitarian architecture where the major function is environmental enjoyment and aesthetic pleasure. The project involves the creation of an environment incorporating man-made images and natural controlled planting, laid out as a domestic garden focussed around a swimming pool.

The basic influencing parameters considered in the overall design approach were the two existing areas of the earlier garden layout; the house and Ikebana Studio designed by the architect in 1966 (the architect's wife, to whom the garden is dedicated, is a professional Ikebana professor and a KOMON graduate). The garden measures in the region of 400 square metres. It consists of various elements woven into an integral whole which are held together by the central pool as a visual focus. The basic construction materials utilized throughout are pre-cast concrete block and local Maltese limestone.

Many of the individual elements such as the masonry Memory Wall and the timber Memory Screen reflect the architect's interest at that time in space-time relationships. Both of these elements portray and evoke time equations. The main sculpture feature is a Victor Pasmore mural installed in 1997.

This is a space mapped out to enable one to rediscover in contemporary terms the usefulness of the useless. It is an environment of stone and nature conceived in the canescent moods of a Mahler adagio: a sacred-meditative space made in De Chirico type atmospheres. It appears as a selection of primary geometries woven into a Theatre of Memory to form an escapist dream world: a space to be sensed not only by the eyes but more so by the soul, a place of magic and meaning, in which to stop and pause, be silent and unspoken to; an architecture where the floor is the earth, the walls are the wind and the ceiling the sky.

This project, together with the Church of St. Joseph Manikata, was awarded the Gold Medal of the City of Toulouse and the Interarch Laureate Prize in 1985.

Bottom, night view of pool area.
Below, site plan of the garden

1. Theatre of Memory
2. Waters of Reflection
3. Memory Wall
4. Temenos
5. Secret Garden
6. Pinnacle of Peace
7. Staircase of Desire
8. Sentinels of Space and Time
9. Garden of Quintessence
10. Cloisters of Remembrance
11. Scented Garden
12. Fountain of Laments
13. Pyramid of Transcendence
14. Memory Screen
15. Steps of Sagacity
16. Hermitage of Solitude
17. Ikebana Studio
18. Goddess of Youth
19. Bar
20. Toilets

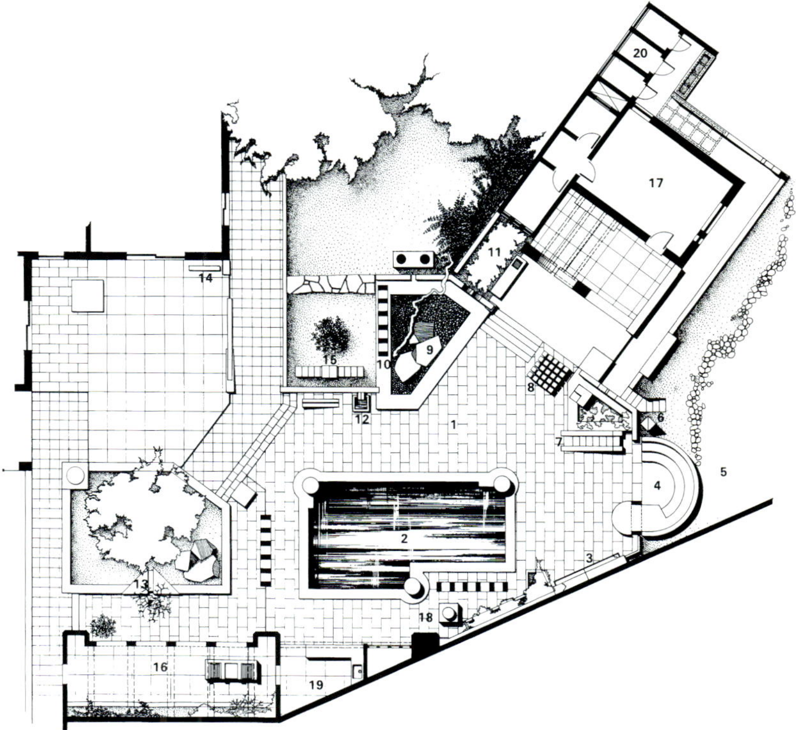

The Memory Wall.

The pool area.
Waters of Reflection.

The portico delimiting the pool, towards the Pyramid of Transcendence and the Hermitage of Solitude.

The Goddess of Youth, near the pool.

The Staircase of Desire, leading to the Pinnacle of Peace.

Aquasun Lido

St. Julians, Malta
1984

"Man dies when the last part of the child in him becomes an adult."

Michael Ende

The Aquasun Lido architecture seeks an expression which invites the participation of its users on many levels and provides a form of stepping stone or threshold for man to walk through into an area of relaxation and recuperation. This is a tourist centre arena built and orchestrated in childhood images, yet belonging to a concrete tangible reality. Its forms and layout evoke the intimacies and social functionalism of traditional Mediterranean village squares, but above all, it is, a creation based on a series of deeper recollective images which work to free frozen memories of one's lost dreams of childhood. This is an architecture of primal imagery, drawing its roots and inspiration from basic house-temple prototypes and in its layers of quintessence its forms relate to the evolution of the whole making of architecture. The geometric relationships of its archetypal forms relate to the origins of architecture in their earliest evolutionary forms.
The basic prototype of the Hut evolving to Temple emerges in the order and hierarchy of this place. These are images which not only relate to the origins of man's first established forms as a builder, but which function on our psyche to recollect individual "remembered things" from our youth, for as Gaston Bachelard has taught us, "it is the child in man that holds the essential key to our whole existence."

Aimed and organized, at the rediscovery of the child dormant within each of us, the Aquasun Lido is conceived as an illusory stage to revive childhood dreams: a stage to search for infant memories to retrace and revive the laughter of one's youth. The main object here, is to enchant, for the world of today, through its sterile imagery, has long lost the potential and meaning of enchantment. Since we cannot actually return to our childhood for rejuvenation, we can at least attempt to find an invented one. The Aquasun Lido spaces are meant as as environmental exercise channeled in the direction of this discovery.

This project was awarded the Commonwealth Association of Architects Regional Award in 1987 and the Georgia, USSR Biennale Laureate Prize in 1988.

The Island of Pontikonissi, Corfu, Greece, one of the sources of inspiration for the Aquasun Lido.

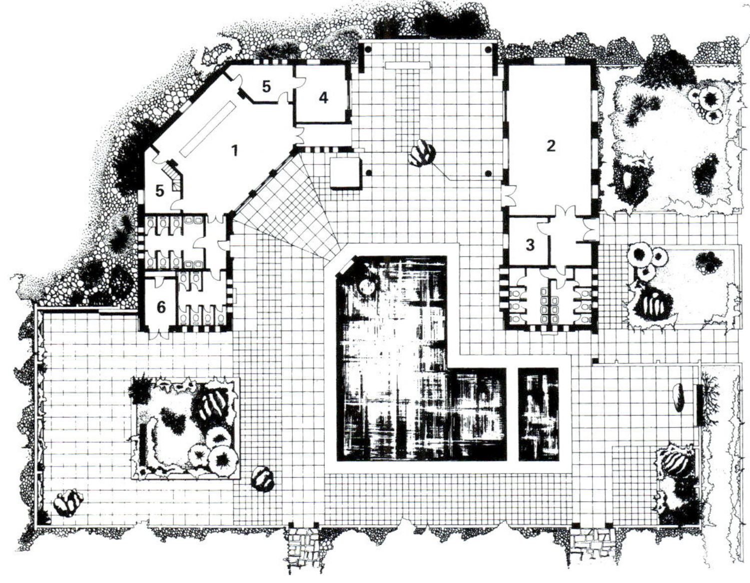

Site plan and, below, night view of the tourist centre.

The archetypal forms surrounding the pool of the Aquasun Lido evoke traditional Mediterranean village squares.

Left, detail of facade facing pool.
Below, entrance hall.

Papal Pavilions

Malta
1990

"I think joy is the key word in our work."

Louis I. Kahn

On the occasion of Pope John Paul II's visit to Malta in May 1990, a number of public ceremonies were scheduled in order to enable the participation of the massive crowds which would attend these events. Richard England was commissioned by the Ecclesiastical Authorities to design the Stands to be used during the public Masses and gatherings celebrated on this occasion. In contrast to the architect's body of private meditative spaces, these projects demonstrate the architect's opulent handling of extensive public sacred gathering places. Richard England has always believed that in a sense these Stands function primarily as temporary stage-sets set up for specific occasions of celebration and pageantry.

Thus the final built-forms are transient colourful settings, choreographic back-drops for the ceremonies celebrated on their stages.

It is interesting to note that the technology utilized for these temporary "buildings" is still the traditional masonry grammar; illustrating that stone technology on England's native island is still very much a living process, and the most economically viable.

The usable life-span of these designs was that of a mere number of hours, but their memory has since outlived their transient existences.

The three Stands received the Interarch Laureate Prize in 1991.

Concept sketch for the Papal stand at Floriana.

The Papal stand
at Floriana.

The Papal stand
at Ta'Qali Stadium.

The Papal stand
at Mellieha.

Sacred Spaces

Malta
1978 - 1996

"Materialistic space transcends itself into sacred space when it becomes a sanctuary for the soul."

Richard England

Richard England's search for an architecture of the spirit is manifest in a body of religious buildings where secular architectural tools are supplemented by the sacred tool of faith. The most sublime problem which an architect can tackle is the creation of a sacred space conducive to prayer. Religious architecture throughout prehistory and history has always been a reflection of man's understanding of the Divine. Current theology has always formed the basis of man's attempt to provide spaces of worship where he could pray to the divinities of the times.

In today's age, where the materialistic has overcome the spiritual, where, despite scientific knowledge man still knows least about what matters most, man's need for contact with the Divine becomes an even more imperative and essential tool for his whole spiritual survival. Richard England argues that therefore such places of solace should also be placed in everyday living environments and habitats. If faith is the ultimate tool in the manifestation of these spaces, simplicity and reverence are the stepping stones to manifest their built-form. The methodology of the architect in the making of these arenas of prayer is reflected in his words:

In the creation of Sacred
Architecture, an architect must seek
to achieve

places of silence
in spaces of solitude
enclosed by walls of mysticism.

The silence attained
must be one that speaks
not muted.

The solitude raised
should be one of communion
and not loneliness.

These works reflect dialogues with absence in order to create exulted forms of silence. This in turn nourishes togetherness and spiritual awareness. Without doubt, religious architecture requires a strong sense of sensitivity on the part of the architect in creating environments conducive to contemplation and meditation. In these works, in contrast to man's everyday monotonous and repetitive locations, Richard England designs his prayer spaces pregnant in mood and meaning. The problem of tackling the concept of sacredness, promoting the recognition of a place as divine, is perhaps still the most challenging design problem that an architect can face. It was Gaudí who said, "the greatest challenge for an architect remains the church".

It is obvious in viewing Richard England's Sacred Spaces that he puts love and commitment into them. He often quotes Mother Teresa "It is not what we do, it is how much love we put out in the doing", in emphasizing that a space can only give back what it receives in its making. This body of works illustrate the architect's subtle sensitivity and spiritual qualities. They are in the words of Mario Pisani "a collection of works which stands comparison with the finest examples of religious architecture in history."

The Franciscan Minor Conventuals' Meditation Chapel at Burmarrad and the M.U.S.E.U.M. Chapel at Blata l-Bajda were awarded the International Prize at the III Costa Rica Biennale in 1996.

Richard England
in his family chapel
at St. Julians, 1993.

The Meditation Chapel,
Society of Christian
Doctrine (M.U.S.E.U.M.),
Blata l-Bajda, 1989.

Chapels at Addolorata Cemetery.
Opposite page, Franciscan Meditation Chapel, Burmarrad, 1996.

Meditation Chapel, Society of Christian Doctrine (M.U.S.E.U.M.) at Naxxar, 1978.
(*Photo*: Carmel H. Psaila)

Chapel of St. Andrew

Pembroke, Malta
1988

"Buildings are also homes for our souls."

Ulrik Plesner

Immediately after the Second World War in the mid-forties, a number of German prisoners of war were stationed in Malta. Among the various activities given to them during that period was the building of a small chapel to serve the community of the British soldiers stationed in army barracks in an area known as St. Andrew's (now Pembroke), not far from the Grand Harbour area of Valletta.

With the departure of the British troops from Malta in 1979, the chapel fell into disuse and abandon. During the late eighties the former military zone was converted into a housing area for local residents with the addition of many new buildings. With the growing number of people, the parish priest of the larger St. Julians parish which incorporated this new residential zone, commissioned Richard England to restore and re-design the abandoned carcass of this building. The architect's initial concept was to create a welcoming space to greet the people before they enter the church itself, while retaining the original structure. An amalgamation of pure geometric forms in strong Mediterranean tones recall the traditional "piazza areas" of this region. In this limited walled space which acts as a threshold between secular and sacred there is a strong juxtaposition of primary shapes and rich colours which evoke the Island's traditions of multi-coloured fishing boats, opulent baroque interiors and chromatic festa-night fireworks.

In contrast, the interior is a simple, evocative place of silence; an area of meditation and an arena of prayer. Within these walls echoing the aftermath of hatred and war, the architect has tried to create a fullness of peace to re-unite man primarily with himself and also with his fellow brotherhood.

This project was awarded an IFRAA - American Institute of Architecture Award for Religious Architecture in 1990.

Interior view of the chapel.

The "welcoming space" in front of the entrance of the restored chapel recalls the traditional "piazza areas" of the region.

In this limited walled space, people can meet at the threshold between secular and sacred spaces.

Private Villa

Malta
1994

"Light is the animator of space through geometry."

Richard England

In this private villa situated in the South East of the Island, the plan closes in onto the exuberant sculptural play of the walled back garden surrounding the pool area. This four bedroomed house with adjacent office offers a rich array of Mediterranean imagery. The massing of the whole is conceived by recodifying original archetypes and models and abstracting traditional forms into a valid contemporary expression.
This habitat also reflects the architect's current flamboyant use of colour to further emphasize his strong formal visual language. Rewarding visual sequences through a variety of multi-transitional interior spaces provide processional walk-throughs into the walled garden environment. Like a spider England attaches a thread to tradition and attempts to spin his own web. A web tied to the earth searching for past roots, reaching out to the future but always anchored to place-time co-ordinates.

As in all his works, one can note the architect's selective process of absorption of International influences into local traditions while still using the ethnic vernacular as a base start. It is this Bartok-like cross fertilization, in the process of abstracting and re-interpreting vernacular elements, in consonance with International overlays and the spirit of our times that earmarks England's creative process as a *valid* regional expression. Richard England has always believed that one must build on the past and not cannibalize it, but the past which he uses as a stepping stone is always one that partains specifically to the locality and place he is building in. Man in fashioning shelter for himself, be it clothes or architecture, has no option but to adopt different solutions for different locations.

Concept sketch.

Below, view of the pool in the interior court. Right, detail of the facade facing the pool.

Opposite page, detail of the side wall of the pool. The use of colour emphasizes the strong formal visual language adopted in this project.

Details of the porch facing the pool.

Ir-Razzett ta' Sandrina

Mgarr l/o Ghajn Tuffieha, Malta
1988 - 1993

> "If there are many equally valid technical solutions to a problem, the one which offers the user a message of beauty and emotion, that one is architecture."
>
> *Luis Barragan*

A converted farmhouse on the North West part of Malta with exceptional views over the countryside and surrounding sea.

The back part of the structure is dug out into the solid rock of the rising hill. The main new design feature was the creation of a central open to the sky space, introvert and private, which enables the owners, a young family to distance themselves from the reality of the fast pace and materialistic demands of everyday life. This arena of surreal poetry consisting of earth, wall and sky, is conceived in pale-colour spectrum combinations of flush pinks and subtle blues. These walls and forms define the tensions between the aerial and the terrestrial. Evocative of spaces of fairy tales, myths and legends, the whole is designed as a stage for dreaming; an enchanting theatre of pure geometry providing a canvas intermix of reality and dream, dominated by the evocative immensity of the release of the sky above. This is a private arcadia steeped in mysticism enclosed by walls of fable and roofed over by wind-blown migrant clouds. It seems somehow appropriate to create such a castle-like space on an island like Malta, strategically perched in the Middle sea at the cross roads of the European fashion of Baroque trompe l'oeil ceilings and the Islamic tradition of lapis-lazuli domes of the near East.

The Magritte, De Chirico, Delvaux iconography of the main open court leads to the more playful area of the smaller court. Here the tower forms of the mural sculpture evoke fantasies of abodes of princesses, regal palaces and castles to be conquered. This is the children's play court, again introvert and protected in physical and spatial terms but infinite in its imaginative possibilities in the mind of the ever dreaming child.

The Pool Area

The pool is constructed on an elevated viewing platform with views of the country side and the sea. The screen wall defining its south facade is punctured to allow views of the distant skyline. Reflections play visual games as these defining walls appear at times clear, at times agitated in their mirrored water images. The whole provides a pavilion for family entertainment and functions as the children's main play-area.

The Chapel

Small and secret, the Meditation Chapel is hollowed out of the rock of earth. It is an attempt to achieve harmony of space through beauty of form. Here an ascetic and monastic treatment is woven on a theme of minimalist architecture to help the user in his or her search to find man's place and location in space and time. Perimeter walls map out the parameters of an intermediate gravel area which in turn defines the stone prayer-mat area. The rough stone spalls mark the necessary transition between the sacred and secular. Sounds of stone and choruses of colours entwine to orchestrate the quiet yet intense silence of this space. The pre-existing rock-hewn major container evokes the island's first religious subterranean spaces and points towards a "return to the womb" path in the architect's attempt to establish a sense of sanctity in this place. This mystical ambiance is further enhanced by the deliberate gesture of foregoing electricity and opting instead only for warm caressing candle light. Against the backdrop of these austere walls, wearing rich ecclesiastical tones, hangs an empty cross, more a symbol of Christ's resurrection than His death. This is the sole applied decorative element in the whole chapel. The serene quality of this space provides a comforting arena of solitude and silence.

Plan and concept sketch.
Below, courtyard stairs.

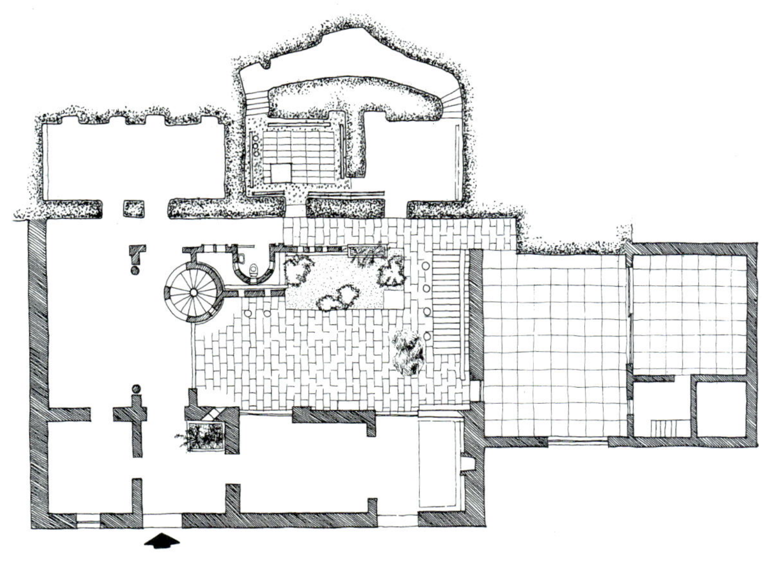

Detail of the exterior stairway and, left, the screen wall defining the south side of the pool terrace.

The pool, constructed on an elevated platform with views of the countryside, offers an interesting play of reflections of the defining walls.

Above, detail
of the castle-like image
of the stair tower.

The meditation chapel.

Dar Il-Hanin Samaritan

Santa Venera, Malta
1996

"Pursue an architecture of memory
or perhaps a memory of architecture."

Richard England

Many of England's projects in the eighties took up the theme of the city in miniature.

The programme for Dar Il-Hanin Samaritan, an old peoples' home in Santa Venera, gave the architect his best opportunity to create an architecture based on memory and nostalgia for times past. In an inward looking u-shaped complex, nostalgia is deliberately encouraged through the skilful use of the repertoire already utilized in A Garden For Myriam and the Aquasun Lido in terms of memory screens and walls. Here they take the form of Baroque doorways marking key points of transition from one part of the complex to the other. Other fragments of a by-gone age are utilized to provide the users with familiar scenarios of their previous life patterns in the urban built-form ambiances of the Maltese villages.

The whole evokes a melancholy world where "the past is a prologue" and the old can find peace and comfort with their remembrances. The composition is rich and opulent but the central courtyard suggests the dreamy urban townscapes of a Mediterranean way of life. The Memory Screen of the Chapel functions as a semantic sign and clearly states "church" while the chapel itself, a subdued cubic structure, is internally washed in a tranquil blue light produced through the filters of locally made glass blocks.

From his early unitary architecture the architect here passes on to a more complex multi-dimensional environment of dream-like forms. Playfulness, disquiet and tranquillity comprise a surreal triad of overlapping ambiguity to produce an expression which is rich and complex but always fascinating. England has stated that "this is a place to be discovered and deciphered, not solely to be viewed."

Richard England has asked that his admiration for Lolly Vella "the most exceptional stone craftsman I have ever met" be here documented. Lolly Vella was responsible for the construction of this complex. He was also the builder of the M.U.S.E.U.M. Chapels in Blata l-Bajda and Naxxar.

Richard England has often said that "working with Lolly puts me in a position where I have serious doubts whether my designs are worthy of his craftsmanship".

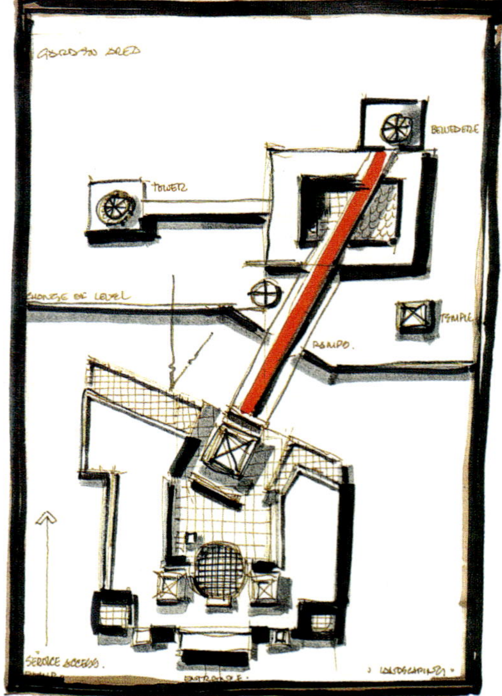

Concept sketch
of the central part of
the religious complex.

Lower ground floor.

1. Chapel
2. Library/lounge
3. Lift
4. Staircase
5. Toilets
6. Service entrance
7. Kitchen and Store
8. Laundry
9. Dining area
10. Craft making
11. Workshop
12. Units
13. Sacristry
14. Meditation garden
15. Way of the Cross
16. Infirmary
17. Reception
18. Administration
19. Night Nurse
20. Entrance
21. Telephone
22. Store
23. Pond
24. Pavilion
25. Village Piazza

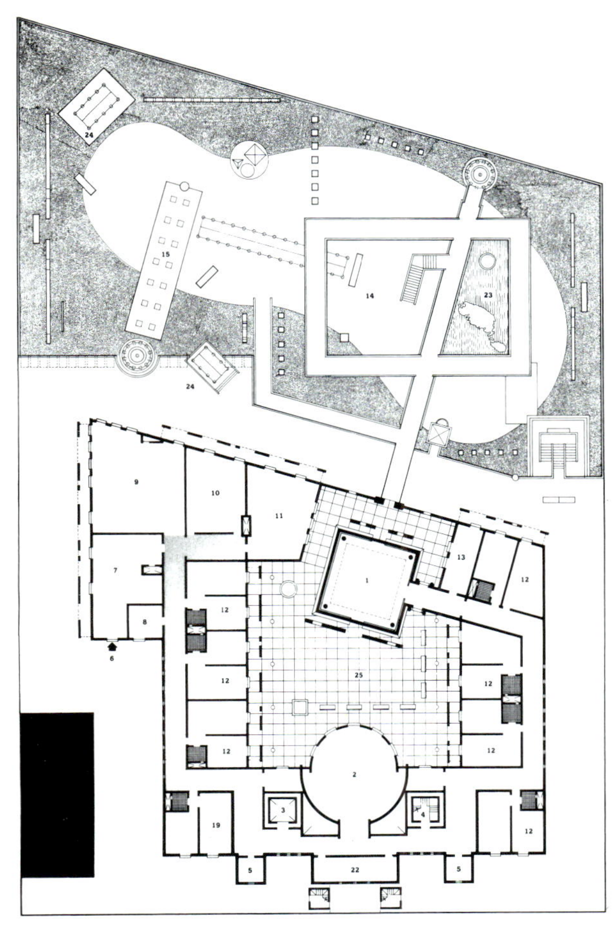

Night view.

The Baroque entrance doorway.

The central courtyard suggesting the urban townscapes of a Mediterranean way of life.

The Baroque screen in front of the cubic volume of the chapel.

Right, the Chapel-screen.
Opposite page,
detail of Baroque
gateway.

The Chapel interior
washed in light through
filters of glass blocks.

Central Bank of Malta

St. James Counterguard, Valletta, Malta
1993

"An architect should mix the tenses of the site."

Richard England

The offices for the Central Bank of Malta are situated within the historical environment of the outer Counterguard bastions of Malta's capital city of Valletta. The preservation and conservation of the 16th Century fortifications were the vital element considered in the design of this project. The new building is "plugged into" the bastion walls so that in no place does it project above the fortification lines. In this manner, it is ensured that the building does not protrude externally above the ancient walls and is only visible from above. The original bastion is retained intact and the new building, conceived as a separate almost removable entity, is carefully lowered and placed into the space defined by the old walls themselves.

The separation between old and new is emphasized by a service and fire escape corridor thus enabling "old" and "new" to be read as individual and different elements. This project probably best demonstrates England's belief in an expression of eco-architecture. It has long been his creed that the quality of an architect is more dependent on his faith in tradition than on his arrogance of revolt. He has always maintained that architecture should vary according to place just as fruit varies according to the soil in which it is planted. This building features both a sense of continuity between the past and present and a synthesis of place and time.

In all his works, England has attempted to follow a philosophy where, in order to design what shall be, one must first of all understand and ultimately protect what has been. The project is deeply rooted in situation, history and local culture, together with a strong sense of belonging to the cultural identity of place. The delicate "insertion" of the new into the old could be likened to a surgeon's task of carefully grafting new tissue onto existing skin. What finally emerges is an almost singularity of concept forged by the interaction of built-form and pre-existent site. In a way, this building is a manifestation of T.S. Eliot's words "the past is altered by the present and the present is directed by the past". In the process of respecting the sensitive historical context of the new building the architect extends his role of designer of the future into that of also being the defender of the past. This process of integration also provides an essential new breath of life to what was before a derelict and unused part of the City.

The actual building process of the Bank premises provided an interesting technical methodology of approach. Since the site had only limited access, it became necessary to first of all lift the initial machinery into place, excavate down between the defensive walls, and then utilize the excavated material to construct a ramp down to the ditch between the counterguard and the city walls themselves. This ramp was then used to provide access for, not only further construction machinery utilized, but also for the delivery of building materials. After the completion of works the ramp was removed.

The building itself consists of three polygonal floors, bounded by the pre-existent walls, at the centre of which is situated a large atrium defined by a glass curtain-wall system which provides ample light and ventilation to the surrounding office spaces.

These three levels are linked by staircases and lifts, while the lower basement houses the Bank's strongrooms and security areas.

The main banking hall incorporates a sculpture relief wall by the eminent British artist Victor Pasmore, who is resident in Malta.

While internally the spaces, equipped with the latest systems of technology, provide comfortable and functional contemporary solutions, externally the building pays a respectful homage to its historical context.

The amalgamation of these two approaches provides a dialectic between the universal and the particular; a synthesis of tradition with comforts and utilities made available by the progress of industrial civilization.

Longitudinal section.

1. Ditch
2. St.James Counterguard

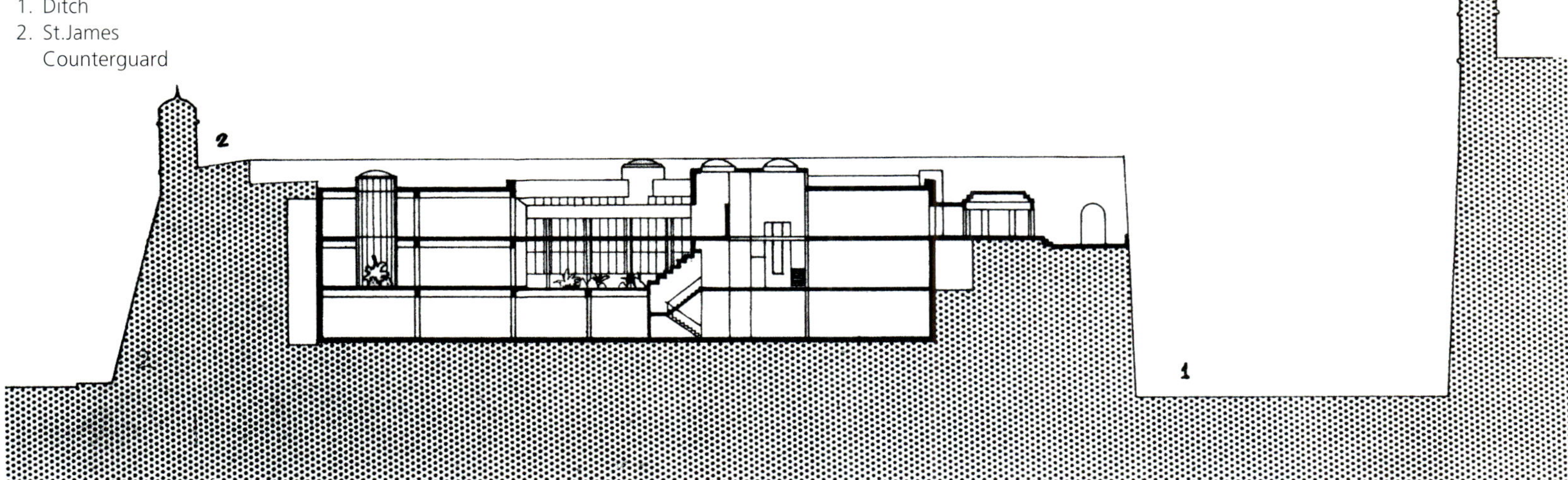

First basement plan.

1. Library
2. Main conference room
3. Research
4. Audit
5. Supervision
6. Finance
7. Human resources

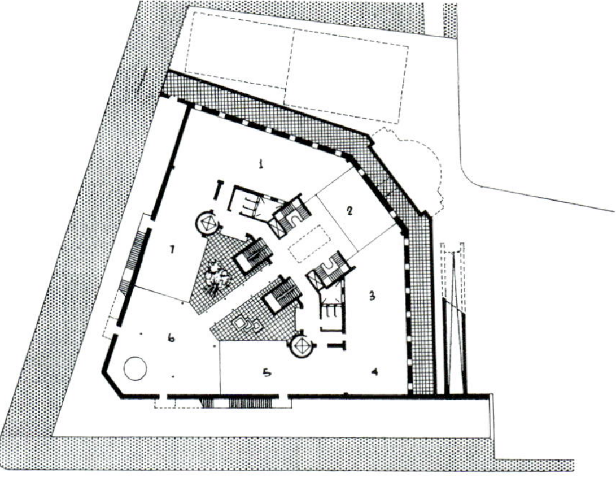

Ground floor plan.

1. Exchange control
2. Banking
3. Foreign
4. Administration
5. Conference rooms
6. Fire escape
7. Plant
8. Existing chapel
9. Pedestrian access
10. Ramp to 2nd basement
11. Stairs to roof
12. Garden

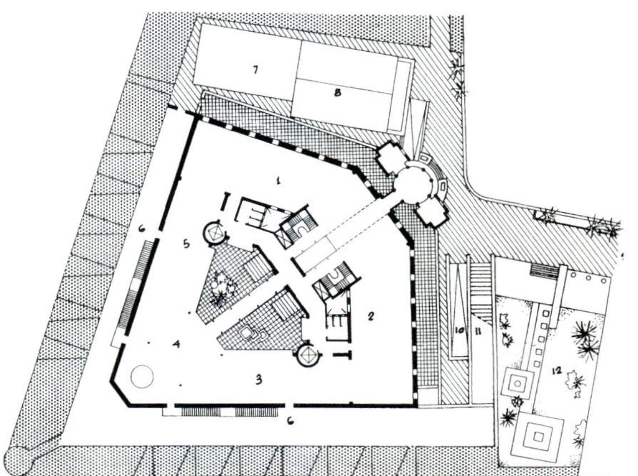

Bird's eye view of complex.

Concept sketch and, below, aerial view of the Bank.

The old and the new in the bastion garden, below detail of the entrance porch.

Opposite page, fountain in internal courtyard.

The exterior ramps to the roof link the new polygonal building to the pre-existing walls. The exterior of the complex pays homage to its historical context.

Right, detail of the interior staircase with, on the left, Victor Pasmore's relief sculpture.
Opposite page, view of the main entrance hall. The interior spaces are equipped with the latest systems of technology and provide comfortable and functional solutions.
Below, entrance porch interior.

University of Malta Extension

Tal-Qroqq, Malta
1989 - 1998

"Architecture is a journey through the past, present and future."

Richard England

The vast extension of the campus of the University of Malta was initiated in 1989 under the Rectorship of Rev. Prof. Peter Serracino Inglott. The original complex was designed in the early sixties by the British firm of architects, Norman + Dawburn. These consisted of a series of slit-windowed, typical of the period, masonry constructions clustered around a central Auditorium Hall which acted as a pivot for the whole layout. The total fabric of this last colonial building complex on the Island presented a not indifferent imported model, one which was well suited to regional conditions and also to the educational requirements of the time. The extension programme, necessary because of the vast increase in the number of students, consists of a series of buildings housing various large lecture halls and particular faculty buildings including that of Architecture and Engineering. Located on the North West part of the campus, the area in question terraces down and forms the border between the existing built-up area and the fertile valley below.

The major formal considerations for the new buildings were in the direction of creating a visual link between the natural unbuilt area below and the pre-existing built elements at the higher level. The new part had therefore to be designed very much in relation to the whole, following Eero Saarinen's advice "always design a thing by considering it in its larger context: a chair in a room, a room in a house, a house in an environment, an environment in a city plan". The concept was to insert a series of new blocks which not only echoed the existing topography but also brought into play the earlier buildings themselves; a process which "builds the site", to borrow a phrase from Mario Botta.

The forms of this cluster focus on an animated series of processional spaces which, through the layering of space and light, give rise to intriguing urban contexts and scenographies. In this layout the spaces between the buildings contribute at least as much as the buildings themselves to the overall environment. Internally evocative of sun-washed traditional narrow street townscapes and externally of defensive ethnic Citadel walls, the whole development is conceived on the concept of re-codifying original archetypes and abstracting traditional forms into a valid contemporary expression. There is an attempt to produce, what Chris Abel has defined elsewhere, as a "reciprocity between improved and traditional models and techniques each balancing and conditioning the other."

This process of "place-making" provides the creation of rewarding visual sequences which culminate in specifically focussed social meeting points or nodes. The greater order of the individual buildings themselves together with the meandering lesser one of the covered porticos attempt to bring together a sense of harmony and balance, not only between modernity and tradition in design and technology, but also between man-made settlement and nature. Once again in this project the completed built-form becomes an icon of the collective memory of place. The architectural language is strictly a vernacular one, which amalgamates with the previous colonial interventions in order to produce a synthesis of the indigenous and the imported, cast in a format of localization which reflects the typical hybridization of both past and present architecture to be found on the Maltese Islands.

Concept sketch of the University of Malta extension.
Below, aerial view of the complex with the new buildings in the foreground.

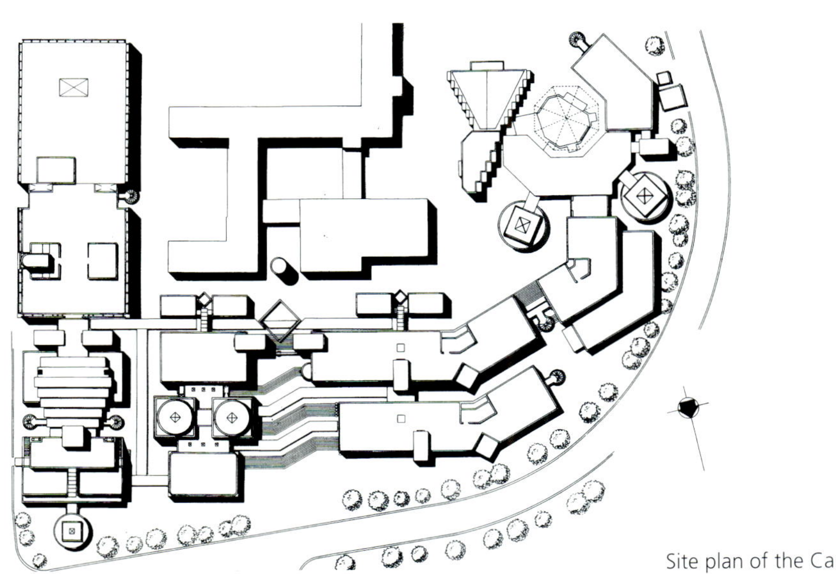

Site plan of the Campus.

Above, overall view.
Right, detail of the staircase to the new entrance of the Campus.

Library and Sculpture Garden.

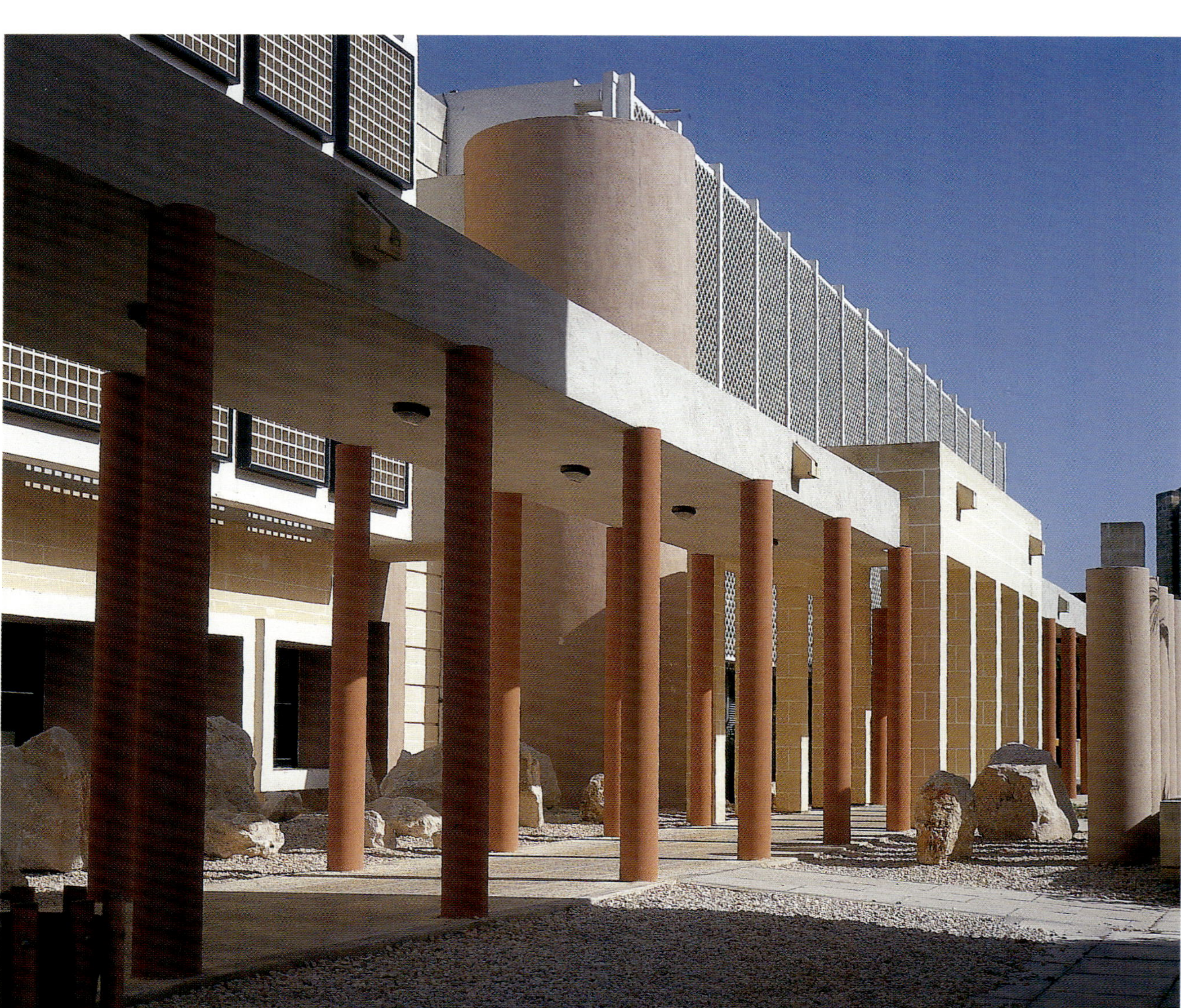

External covered pathways give rise to scenographical urban contexts.

One of the terraced gardens visually connecting the Campus to the valley below.

Externally the Campus
is evocative of defensive
citadel walls.
The central feature
is the water tower.

Detail of the facade and of the stone garden in front of the library.

The entrance hall and exhibition space in the Architecture and Engineering Building in the north-west part of the Campus.

The sequences of built structures and voids create intriguing plays of light and shade.

Church of St. Francis

Qawra, Malta
1988 - 1998

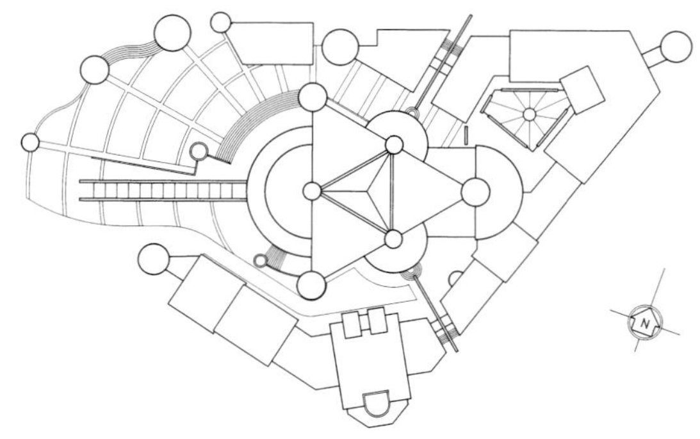

Concept sketch and plan of the church and convent.

"Architecture is in a sense a microcosm of the city."

Denys Lasdun

A large church seating one thousand people together with convent and parish centre planned in a rapidly developing area of Malta. The church and convent comissioned by the Franciscan Fathers (Minor Conventuals) is dedicated to St. Francis of Assisi.

The church is built on a series of strong geometric forms which come together in order to provide a vast internal spatial entity.

Externally the complex is designed in a cascading order from the central church as a main focus to the surrounding ancillary buildings. The interpenetration of the various internal spaces demonstrates England's maturity in handling volumes of considerable size.

The whole has a formal strength which still however manages to reflect a strong sense of the Sacred.

Sketch of interior
and rendering of church
and piazza area.

Left and opposite page, details of the strong massive walls of the religious complex.

General view of the church, built on a series of strong intersecting geometric volumes.

Projects

Bab Al Sheikh Development

Baghdad, Iraq
1982

In the vast early eighties rebuilding programme of the city of Baghdad, Rifat Chadirji, the Iraqi architect, who was the organizer and adviser for the over-all scheme, chose a number of architects to work on one of the largest development schemes of the time. Architects involved in working in Baghdad at that time through Chadirji's invitation included Arup Associates, Ricardo Bofill, Arthur Eriksson, Carlfried Mutcheler, Robert Venturi, Sheppard Robson, TAC and Richard England.

England's work in Baghdad was again a reflection of his life-long philosophy of preserving cultural identity and reinforcing ethnic characteristics through the bringing together in a synthesis "re-coded" traditional forms and new techniques. The architecture of his Middle Eastern projects emerges as a profusion of images in layers of veiled opacity reminiscent of traditional Islamic architecture, with its elaborate screen and shading devices.

The Bab al Sheikh office, perhaps the least Mannerist of England's buildings in Iraq, curves its elegant mass embracing the existing Kheylani Mosque. The building to house offices, conference halls, exhibition spaces and restaurants, has an area of 9,000 square metres.

The problem seemed to focus on trying to adopt a solution to a building which had no traditional archetype. Above all, the building is designed as a backdrop for the existing mosque and is broken down to adhere to the residential scale of the city. Work on the building was started in 1984 but was later abandoned.

Concept sketch
of the office block.
Left, Project for the
Biblioteca Alexandrina,
Egypt, competition entry
1989.

Views of the model.
The office block is clustered around the existing Keylani Mosque, to form a terraced backdrop.

Aerial view of the model. The development has an area of 9,000 sq.m. and is designed to house offices, conference halls, exhibition spaces and restaurants.

House for an Artist

Buenos Aires, Argentina
1986

The project for the house for an artist is a demonstration of an avant-garde architecture where England tackles the project with exuberance taking full opportunity to give full and free reign to his creative imagination.

The plan has all the attributes of a painterly collage, but the main generating idea is once again the breaking down of a single building in such a way that the paths and spaces resemble more an urban than an architectural composition.

The generating form is the image of the walled city. For England the city is the ultimate embodiment of territory and place.

This project becomes, in his hands, a miniature citadel recalling once again the mystic cities of memory of the architect's favourite literary figure Italo Calvino. Within its enclosing walls one can visualise echoes of such mythic and legendary elements as hanging gardens, biblical towers and classical temple pavilions, in addition to the more functional and living spaces.

This is an architecture typical of what Robert Venturi has called "an architecture of complexity and contradiction."

Concept sketch and, right, perspective views of the house.

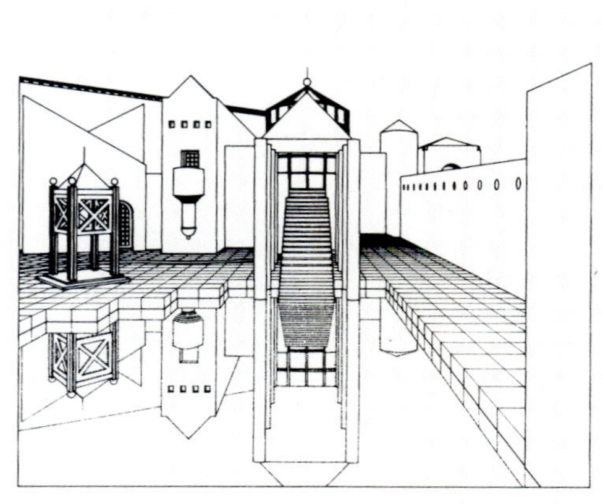

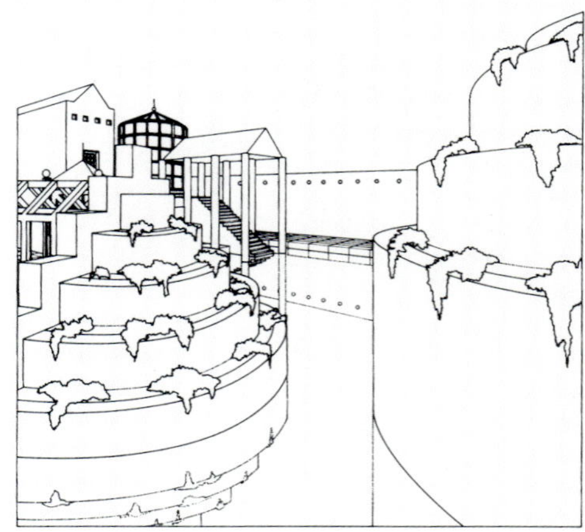

Model of the house. The project breaks down the idea of a single residential building and proposes a series of paths, void areas and volumes resembling an urban composition.

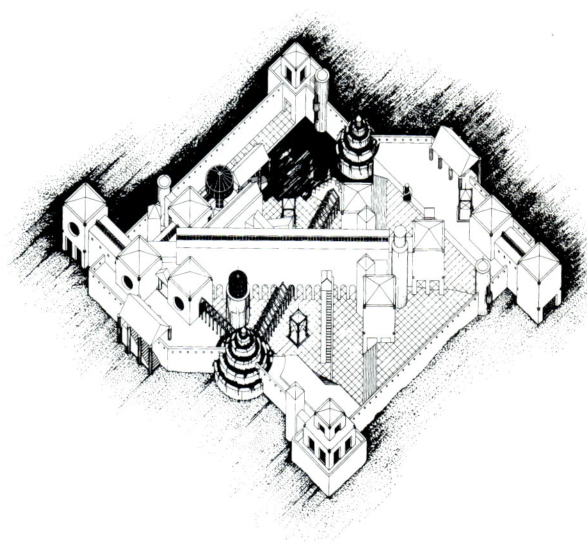

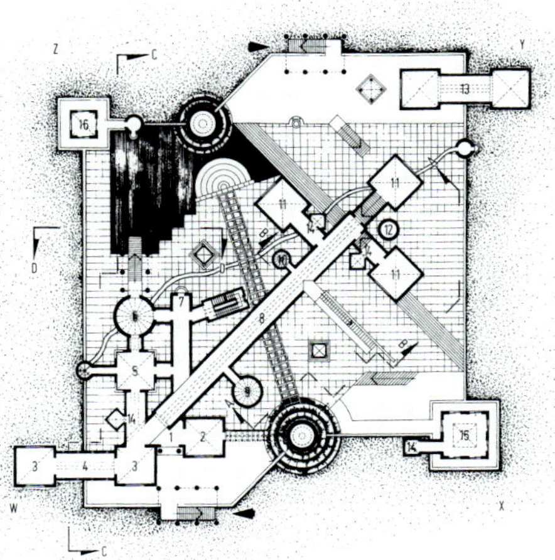

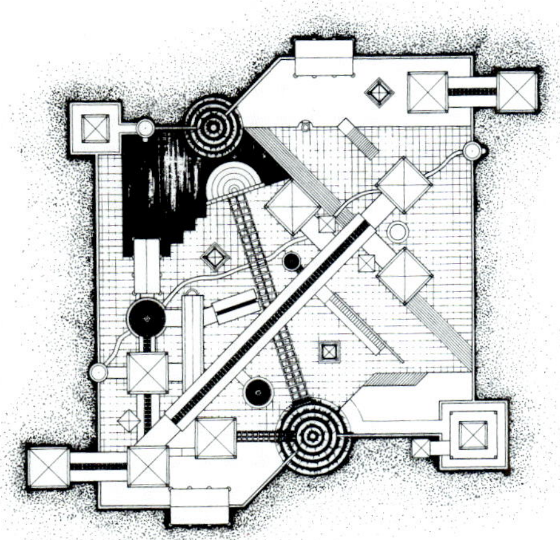

Above, axonometric.
Left, floor plan at + 4.5 m, and roof plan.

1. Entrance
2. Study
3. Living area
4. Library
5. Kitchen
6. Dining
7. Belvedere
8. Exhibition space
9. Sculpture pavilion
10. Viewing pavilion
11. Bedroom
12. Water tower
13. Garage-workshop
14. Lavatory
15. Studio
16. Pool pavilion

Church

Wroclaw, Poland
1987

Axonometric.

A project for a church on the outskirts of the city of Wroclaw in Poland which remained unbuilt.

Typical of England's second phase of metaphysical architecture, it follows on from the ideas developed in A Garden For Myriam and the Aquasun Lido. As in the Dar il-Hanin Samaritan complex, the concept is that of a "city of memory".

The jagged massing with its spires and triangular gable ends bears a remarkable resemblance to old drawings of medieval Polish cities.

On the darker side, the images of war-torn Poland are conjured up by the skeleton-like open frames of the spires. While this is definitely an architecture of ambiguity, the complex composition is skilfully handled and the architect's sense of place and his capacity to relate buildings to site is once again evident.

Concept sketch.

Above, rendering.
Right, floor plan at
+ 2,4 m and block plan.

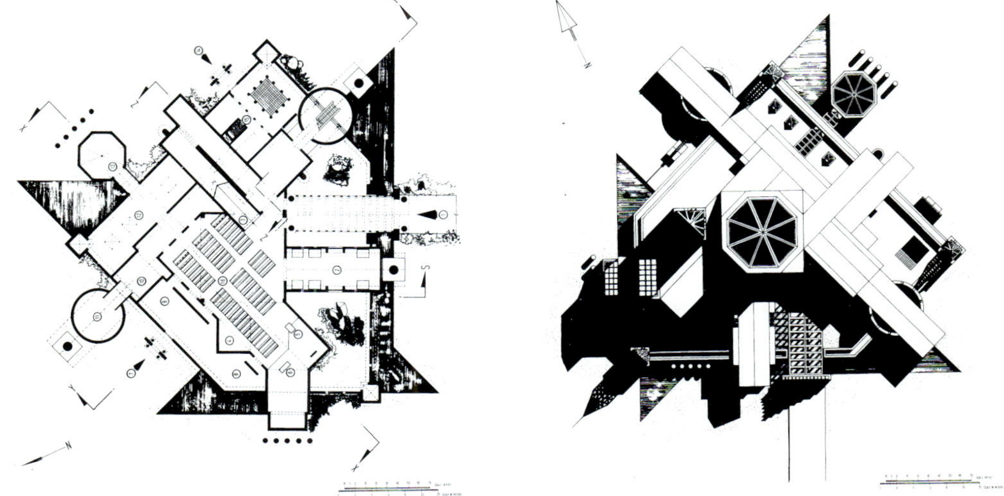

Expo '92 Malta Stand

Seville, Spain
1992

A scheme prepared with Conrad Buhagiar and David Felice for the Malta Stand at the Expo '92 exhibition in Seville.

The building takes its cue from the spiral motifs of Malta's megalithic temples. Visitors are encouraged to walk up the ramp in the cone-shaped tower enjoying a panorama of the Island's history and heritage, to then descend and exit via a lift tower.

The presence of water further enhances the composition of the scheme.

The project, despite being enthusiastically received by the Expo Authorities, remained unbuilt.

Concept sketches of the project which takes its inspiration from the spiral motifs of Malta's megalithic temples.

Apartments, Golf 12

Belgrade, Yugoslavia
1990 - 1997

In 1992, the Yugoslav Veletehna-CIP development company commissioned the architect-critic, Ivica Mladjenovic to select eight architects to design their Golf 12 project incorporating eight different blocks of apartments in Belgrade.

Mladjenovic selected a group of internationally known architects: Justus Dahinden, Stanley Tigerman, Kisho Kurokawa, Klaus Kada, Henry Nielebock, Yacov Rechter, Yugoslav Aleksandar Dokic together with Richard England. Each of these architects presented designs for their projects and construction was started in 1994.

The development is located in the area of Banovo Brdo., Cukarica, one of the highest points in Belgrade, with excellent views of the city. Richard England's building comprises eighteen apartments and manifests his now established Mediterranean methodology of handling masses in strong sculpture interplays of light and shadow.

Concept sketch, plan of typical floor, and front elevation.

House

Moscow, Russia
1994

Concept sketches of the housing complex showing the isolated geometric volumes linked by the sweeping curved blue wall.

In 1994, the International Academy of Architecture selected a number of its Academicians to design a collection of houses for a proposed Moscow Interbau Exhibition.

Richard England's design is a series of isolated geometric volumes linked through a sweeping curved blue wall. The building presents an interesting interplay of spaces and in its totality emerges as the architect's homage to the Russian Constructivist Movement with special reference to Melnikov.

Axonometric.

Perspective view, and below, plan and section.

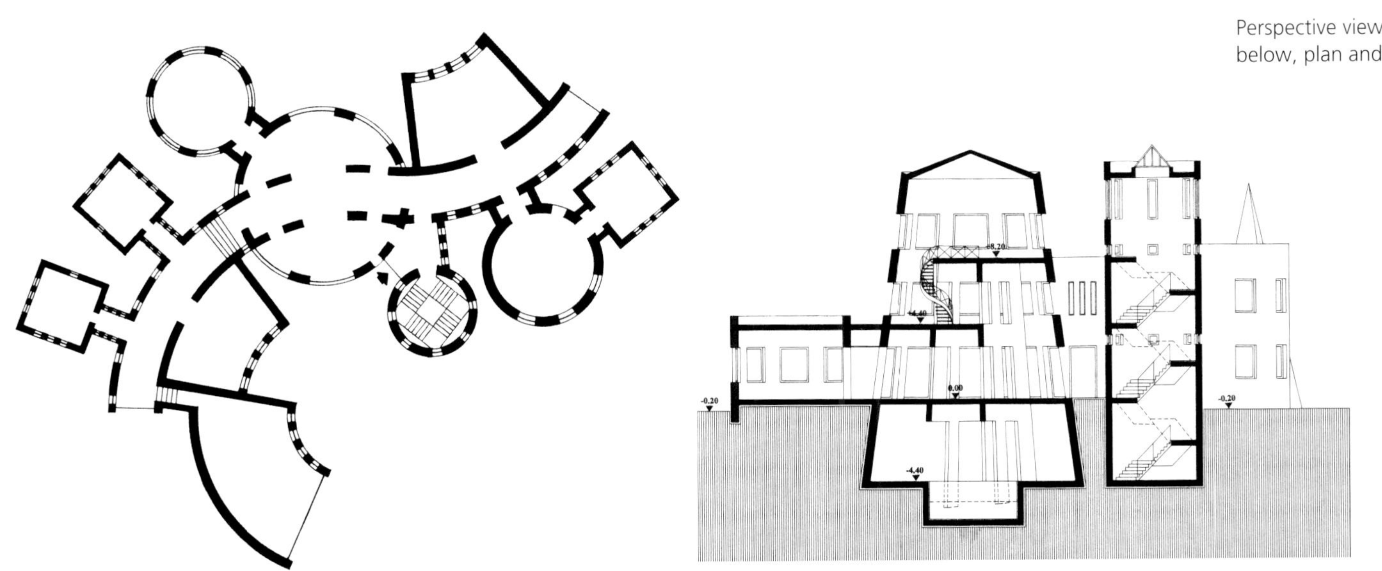

Government Hospital

Tal-Qroqq, Malta
1989 - in progress

A scheme for a new Government Hospital where Richard England acted as design consultant to the Italian OR.TE.SA. spa Group in their capacity as Hospital Designers.

England's external design and massing scheme is formulated in such a way as to combine visually with his adjacent University scheme.

The Hospital houses 475 beds and has an overall area of 40,000 square metres.

Despite its size the complex adheres successfully to the terrain, and because of the breaking down into individual units of the whole echoes the general ethnic building scale of the island.

Concept sketch and, right, axonometric.

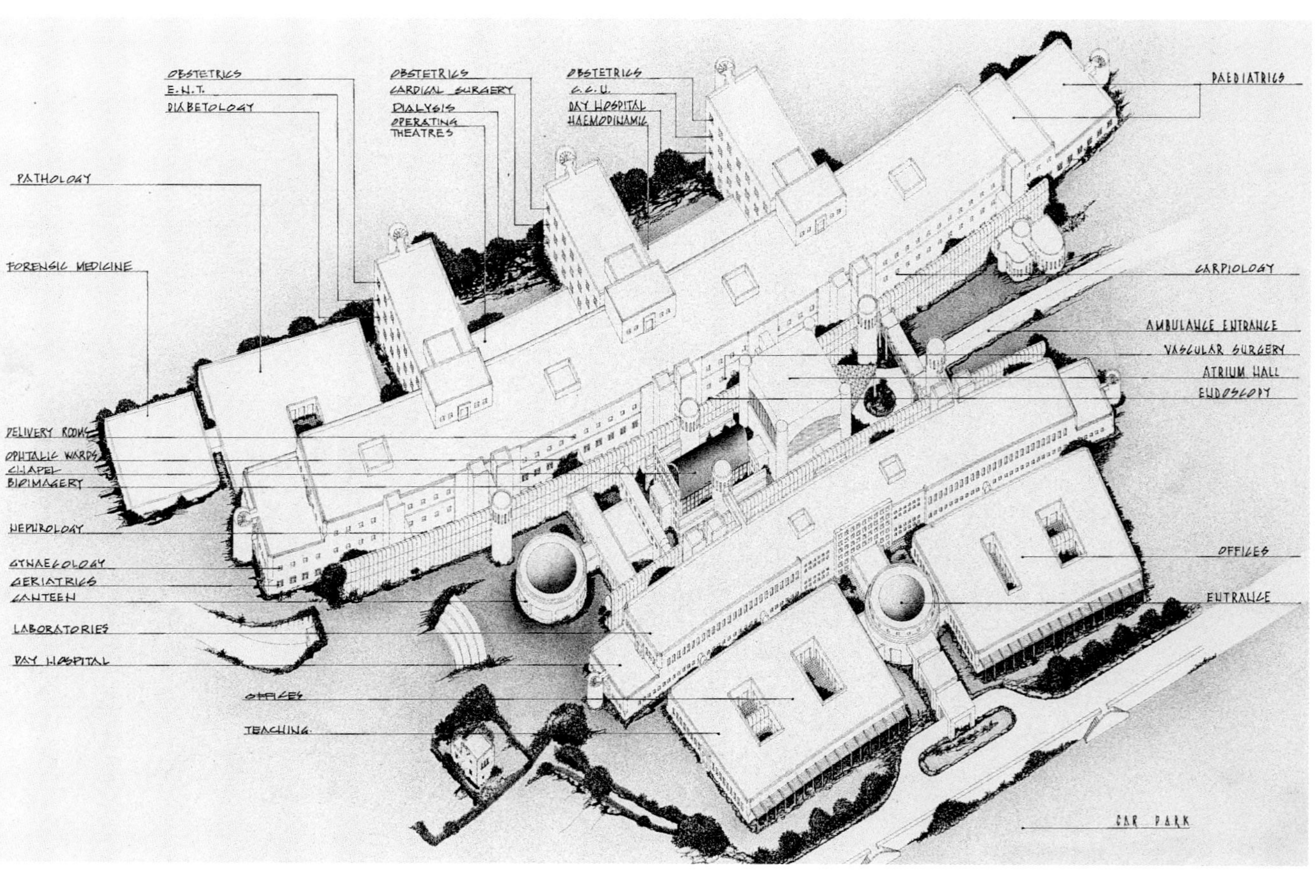

Section and aerial view of the model.

North elevation.

National Arts Centre Phase 1

St. James Cavalier, Valletta, Malta
1996 - 1998

The St. James Cavalier was built in 1566 in order to guard the entrance of the fortified city of the new capital of Malta, Valletta. This bastion or raised artillery platform formed part of the major defensive system for the city as designed by Francesco Laparelli and Girolomo Cassar after the Great Siege of 1565. The Cavalier was later used by Napoleon's troops in 1798, while the British also used it as part of the fortifications which they had taken over in 1800.
A considerable amount of changes and alterations were carried out during this latter period including the addition of an intermediate floor and the installation of two large water-cisterns installed as part of the overall Valletta water supply system.

The Malta Government has now earmarked the Cavalier to form part of the overall scheme of the new National Arts Centre which will also incorporate the new building on the adjacent former Opera House site destroyed in World War II. As Phase One of the manifestation of the Arts Centre, the Cavalier is being restored and rehabilitated to provide a centre which will act as a focus for the Arts and as a stimulus for creativity and participation in various artistic fields. One of the vital problems in this design exercise was the circulation system of visitors within the Centre bearing in mind that the original function of the structure was that of a closed defensive war machine. As such both external access and internal circulation were limited and very much contrary to the scope of the original requirements. Therefore, in order for the Centre to fulfill its new function, it has been deemed necessary to excavate one of the British-built water cisterns to a lower level to provide a vertical circulation system for the whole building. This circular top-lit space will provide a dramatic atrium which accommodates, not only the necessary circulation areas, but also spaces for exhibition and other activities. The National Arts Centre, as an entity, composed of both St James Cavalier and the new building of the old Opera House site, is being envisaged as the prime project in the regeneration and rehabilitation of Valletta.

Once completed, St. James Cavalier will incorporate spaces for visual art exhibitions, workshops, book and record shops, music rooms, jazz cafe, cyber-cafe, cinematheque, cinematheque library, child education facilities and a 150 seat flexible theatre installed in the second of the 19th Century water cisterns. In the remodelling of these 16th Century fortifications, the architect's customary good manners prevail, yet the inserted new elements are made to read specifically as contemporary elements. The whole concept is based on the same philosophy utilized in the Central Bank project of transposing the past into the present so that it may be preserved for the future.

Concept sketch.

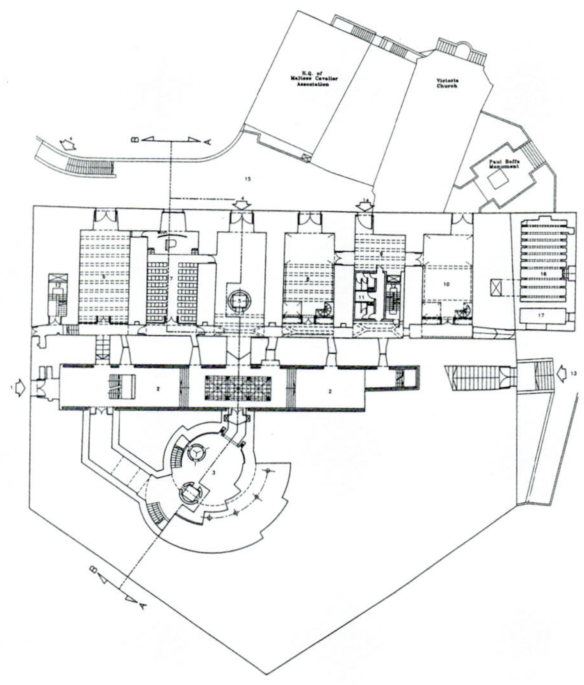

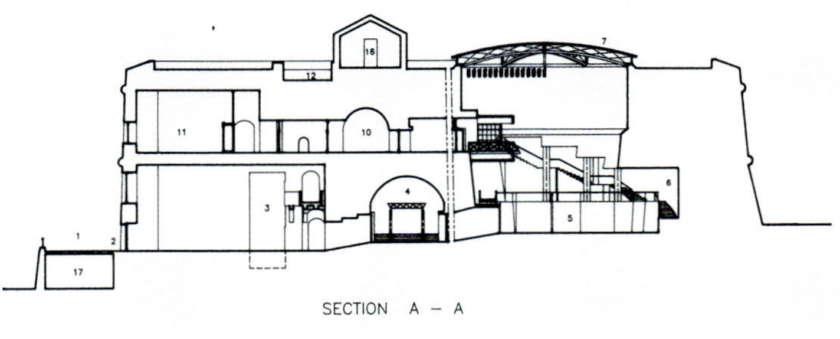
SECTION A – A

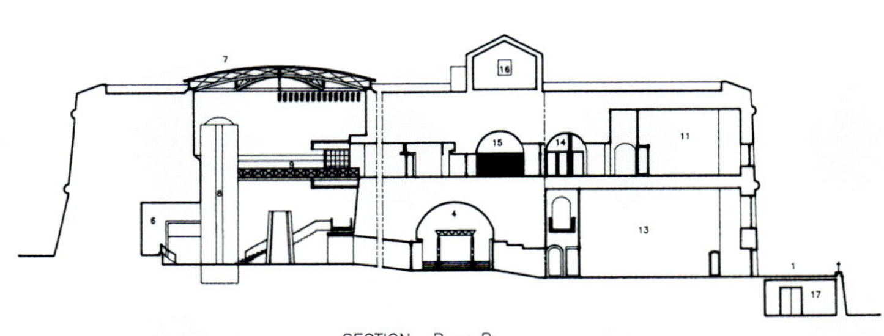
SECTION B – B

Plan of first level.
1. Proposed main entrance
2. Main hall
3. Vertical circulation
4. Night entrance
5. Staff lift
6. Book shop
7. Music room
8. Jazz cafè
9. Kitchen
10. Cyber cafè
11. Public toilets Disabled WC
12. Fire escape stairs
13. Existing entrance
14. Service entrance
15. Outside cafè area
16. Electrical distribution room
17. Existing electrical distribution station

AA section, top, and BB section.
1. Outside cafe area
2. Night entrance
3. Staff lift
4. Main hall
5. Vertical circulation
6. Stairs to theatre
7. Vertical circulation glass roof structure
8. Public lift
9. Bridge link to theatre
10. Stairs from existing entrance
11. Child education facilities
12. Existing ramp roof access
13. Music room
14. Dressing room and toilets
15. Access to roof and maintenance roof
16. A/C Control room
17. Store

Concept sketch of the central part of the Arts Centre.

Main circulation space in one of the old water-cisterns.

National Arts Centre Phase 2

Opera House Site, Valletta, Malta
1992-in progress

The old Opera House at the entrance of Malta's capital city of Valletta was a 19th Century Neo-Classic building designed by Edward Middleton Barry, the architect of the Covent Garden Opera House in London.

The building had a chequered history having been gutted by fire in 1873 re-built and finally destroyed by enemy bombing in 1942. To this day the site has remained a ruin, manifesting a clear sense of recollection as if it were only yesterday that the Luftwaffe had razed it to the ground.

The older generation of Malta speaks of it with a sense of permanent presence and clamours for the re-construction of the building as they knew it.

The younger generation is not so sure of where its loyalties lie.

It has no memory of the building, only photographs and the never-ending stories which their parents relate. The debate as to whether the building should be a replica of Barry's design or a new one continues to this day. In a 1992 local competition no clear winner appeared but the scheme prepared by Richard England with Conrad Buhagiar and David Felice received a special mention from the jury.

The scheme incorporated the proposed re-construction of the front screen of Barry's main facade in a form of a memory screen which linked the present to the past. Behind this facade a glass curtain wall allowed visual links between the capital city's main thoroughfare and the theatre foyer, so that street became foyer and foyer in turn mingled into the street.

In 1995, Richard England was directly commissioned by the Malta Government to design the new Arts Centre on the Opera House site. The building is to be a multi-purpose Arts Centre which incorporates also the rehabilitation of the adjacent St. James Cavalier. The designs being developed by England at present still focus on the reconstruction of Barry's main facade but this has now been moved to behind the curtain wall facade in order to evoke stronger manifestations of a framed past as if encapsulated in a frozen time-frame memory.

The illustrated scheme is the one developed for the competition in 1992.

Sketch, from main square with St.James Cavalier on right hand side.

Axonometric.

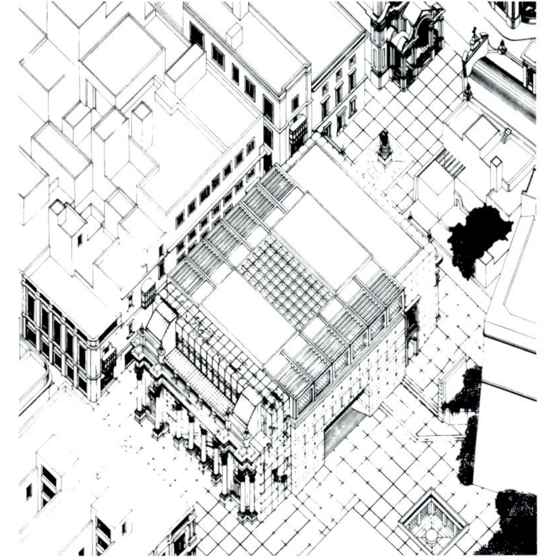

Plan of entrance level and perspective view.
Plan of the auditorium level and perspective view.

Perspective view of the square with the new Arts Centre.
Main square elevation.

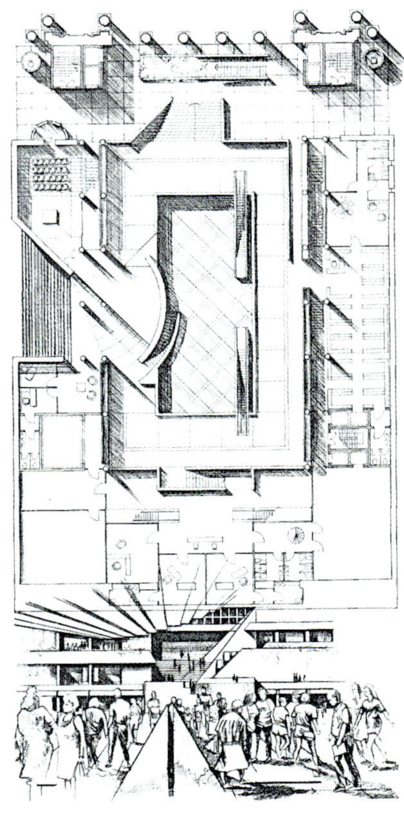

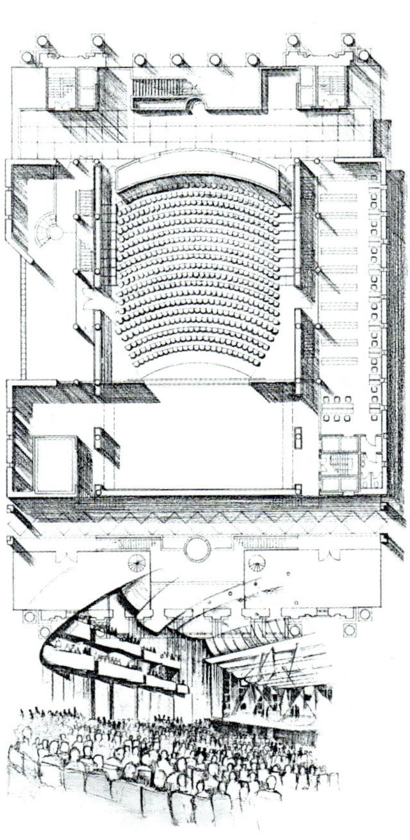

To create an architecture
where the floor is the earth
the walls are the wind
and the ceiling is the sky,
that is my goal.

Richard England

Biography

Richard England was born in Malta and graduated in Architecture at the University of Malta. He continued his studies in Italy at the Milan Polytechnic and also worked as a student-architect in the studio of the Italian architect-designer Gio Ponti.
He is a sculptor, photographer, poet, painter and also the author of several books.
His work has been extensively published in leading international journals, while a number of books have been written on his work.
He has travelled, lectured and exhibited in North and South America, Europe, the Middle and Far East and the ex-U.S.S.R.
Richard England is a Visiting Professor at the University of Malta, a Professor (Honoris Causa) at the University of Buenos Aires, Argentina, and a Visiting Fellow at the University of Bath, in England.
He also was a Professor at the International Academy of Architecture before being appointed Academician in 1991.
He is also a Professor (Honoris Causa) at the Institute of Advanced Studies at the University of New York, U.S.A.
In 1993 the Government of Malta appointed him Officer of The Order of Merit.
In 1995, he was appointed a Professor (Honoris Causa) at the University of the Republic of Georgia.
His buildings and designs have earned him numerous International Awards, including the Interarch 1985 and Interarch 1991 Laureate Prizes and two Commonwealth Association of Architects Regional awards in 1985 and 1987.
Other awards include the Gold Medal of the City of Toulouse in 1985, the "Comite Des Critiques d'Architecture" (C.I.C.A.) Silver Medal in 1987, the 1988 Georgia, U.S.S.R. Biennale Laureate Prize and an IFRAA - AIA Award for Religious Buildings in 1991.
In 1996 he was the winner of the International Prize at the III Architectural Biennial of Costa Rica.
He has worked in the capacity of Architectural Consultant to governmental and private institutions in the following countries: Yugoslavia, Saudi Arabia, Iraq, Italy, Argentina, Poland, Bulgaria, the Ex-Soviet Union, and his native Malta.

Bibliography

Books on Richard England

Richard England, Architect in Malta, Emile Henvaux. Editions de la Libraire Encyclopedique, Brussels, 1969.

Manikata: The Making of a Church, Charles Knevitt, a Manikata Church Publication, Malta, 1980. Second Edition, 1986.

Cards on the Table: Concept Drawings by Richard England, Maelee Thomson Foster, M.R.S.M. Publications, 1980. Second edition, revised and enlarged, 1983.

Connections: The Architecture of Richard England, Charles Knevitt, Lund Humphries, London, 1984.

Transformations: Richard England, 25 Years of Architecture, Chris Abel, Mid-Med Bank Limited, Malta, 1987.

Manikata Church Malta, Chris Abel, Academy Editions, London, 1995.

Richard England's work has been featured in numerous books and architectural periodicals including l'Arca, L'Architettura, Materia, The Architectural Review, The Architect's Journal, Architectural Design, Progressive Architecture, Architectural Digest, A+U, L'Architecture d'Aujourd'hui, etc.

Books by Richard England

Walls of Malta, photo-prose poem, M.R.S.M. Publications, Malta, 1973.

White is White, poems and epigrams, M.R.S.M. Publications, Malta, 1973.

Contemporary Art in Malta, editor and contributor, A Malta Art Festival Publication, Malta, 1974.

Carrier-Citadel Metamorphosis, M.R.S.M. Publications, Malta, 1980.

Island: A poem for seeing, M.R.S.M. Publications, Malta, 1980.

Uncaged Reflections, selected writings 1965 - 80, M.R.S.M. Publications, Malta, 1980.

In Search of Silent Spaces, M.R.S.M. Publications, Malta, 1983.

Octaves of Reflection, with Charles Camilleri, A John Arthur Studio Publication, London, 1987.

Eye to I, selected poems, Said International Limited, Malta, 1994.

Sacri Luoghi, LIBR*i*A, Italy, 1994.

Mdina. Citadel of Memory, with Conrad Thake, Atlantis Publications, Malta, 1995.

Fraxions, LIBR*i*A, Italy, 1995.

Gozo. Island of Oblivion, LIBR*i*A, Italy, 1997.

Concept and Malta Sketches
Richard England

Photo Credits
David Pisani (Cover)
John Arthur Studio (Models)
John Bethall (Early Works)
Simon Brown (Ir-Razzett ta'Sandrina)
Joseph Cassar
Anthony Cassar Desain
Daniel Cilia (Private Chapel page 41)
Richard England

Colour Renderings "Projects" Section
Jock Bevan

Richard England would like to thank all past and present members of his architectural team of England & England for their contributions, especially Albert Borg Costanzi.

He also acknowledges contributions made by the following: Doris Bonello, Paul Borg, John Catania, John Fenech, Mariella Galea, Francis Galea Naudi, Louis Muscat and Alfred Zahra.

Richard England would also like to document his special thanks to Rita Azzopardi an invaluable secretary for the past thirteen years.

Finally, the deepest of gratitude goes to his wife Myriam, his daughter Sandrina and his son Marc for their understanding, patience and constant support throughout his creative career.

For the publication of this monograph Richard England would like to thank Cesare Casati, Pierantonio Giacoppo, Maurizio Vitta and Franca Rottola, together with all the design team at l'Arca Edizioni.

Richard England
England + England Architects
26 Merchants Street
Valletta Malta
Tels: (356) 330171 / 245187
Fax: (356) 334263